Rat Training

Complete Training Made Easy

Rat Training

Complete Care and Training

Miriam Fields-Babineau

COMPANIONHOUSE
B O O K S

CompanionHouse Books™ is an imprint of Fox Chapel Publishing.

June Kikuchi, *Editorial Director*
Douglas L. Coward, D.V.M., *Special Consultant*
Jamie Quirk and Jarelle Stein, *Editors*
Karen Julian, *Publishing Coordinator*
Tracy Burns, Jessica Jaensch, *Production Coordinators*
Amy Stirnkorb, *Designer*
Indexed by Melody Englund
The photographs in this book are courtesy of Virginia Broitman, Jeff Broitman, Samantha Martin, Evan Cohen, Mrs. DiSesso, Miriam Fields-Babineau, iStockphoto, and Carolyn McKeone.

Library of Congress Cataloging-in-Publication Data

Fields-Babineau, Miriam.
  Rat training / by Miriam Fields-Babineau ; photos by Virginia Broitman ...[et al.].
      p. cm. — (Complete training made easy)
  ISBN 978-1-933958-68-2
  1. Rats—Training. 2. Rats as pets. I. Title.

  SF459.R3F54 2008
  636.935'2—dc22
                        2008044235

Fox Chapel Publishing
903 Square Street
Mount Joy, PA 17552

www.facebook.com/companionhousebooks

We are always looking for talented authors. To submit an idea, please send a brief inquiry to acquisitions@foxchapelpublishing.com.

Printed and bound in the United States

Acknowledgments

I WISH TO THANK MY PHOTOGRAPHERS, EVAN COHEN and Virginia Broitman, for their time and efforts in helping me visualize the training techniques through their wonderful talents. It's not easy maintaining the correct lighting and photographing such small creatures as they move about. Virginia, who is also an extraordinary animal trainer, also owned many of the rodent models. She kindly provided the venue for the book's photo session—her house. Evan and Virginia, I couldn't have done this without the two of you.

I also wish to thank my acquisitions editor at BowTie Press, Andew DePrisco, for having faith that this book would be a good subject for publication.

Big thanks also to Samantha Martin and Mrs. Disesso, Moe's widow, for all of their help in the world of rats in media productions.

This book is for my father, Armond Fields, and step-mother, Sara Fields, who asked me one day, "Why not write a rat training book?" as their rats, Ira and Hy, cavorted about them while they sat on their couch. My parents adored their rats and were thrilled with each new behavior they learned. So here it is, Dad and Mom, the book you suggested. I even used Ira as one of the subjects' names.

This book is also dedicated to all the rats, and their train-ers, who have worked in the media. The other rat named in this book is Ben, of the movie *Willard* fame.

Contents

1

Rat Array

When you are looking for a prospective pet, first impressions count.

BEFORE YOU WELCOME A RAT INTO YOUR HOME, make
sure you and your chosen pet are right for each other. Your
choice of a rodent instead of the more common cat, dog, or bird
should be based on a good understanding of rats' social, practical,
and veterinary needs, which may be more like those of other
housepets than you think. Rat ownership is sure to be more fun
and more successful if you plan ahead and can answer yes to the
following questions: Do you want an active, *inter*active pet with
loads of personality? Do you have at least a half hour (and prefer-
ably a couple of hours) each day to care for and play with your
rat? Are you prepared to regularly clean the cage and do occa-
sional rodent refuse duty? If you are an adult in a household with
young children, will you be there to supervise their interactions

with the new pet? Have you made sure no one in your home is allergic to rodents?

So many questions!

If you're reading this book, chances are you're already hooked on rats and have set out to learn as much as you can. Kudos to you! That also means a few of you are willing to rule out rat ownership. For example, if you weren't expecting to clean your rat's cage at least once a week and pick up his droppings when he's out for a stroll around the house, rat keeping is probably not for you. If you intend to buy a rat to give your children a pet that will be easier to tend than other animals, you'll find that rats do not make good pets for small children, who are too young to understand proper handling or rough play. Don't expect to turn over rat care to youngsters. The responsibility for your pet's care and safety is yours alone, and you should be available to supervise all encounters between your rat and the children in the house to prevent unfortunate mishaps for all involved. Finally, if you think a pet rat will be less likely to cause allergic reactions than other animals, you'll find that people with allergies may react to an adult rat even if handling a baby rat (known as a pup or a kitten) doesn't bother them.

If you've done your homework and decided that you are ready to handle the responsibility, congratulations! You'll be welcoming a responsive, intelligent, trainable pet into your home.

Finding the Perfect Rat

Rats are often an impulse purchase. Unfortunately, as with any impulse purchase, the interest in the animal can quickly fade, leaving the rodent to a solitary life with little stimulation, or worse. Don't give in to the impulse; advance planning will

It pays to shop around—rats of all kinds are available to the persistent, discerning buyer.

benefit all parties. To find the perfect rat, check out a few different sources before making your purchase.

Many people go directly to the pet store, as most shops stock rats as reptile food, with a few of the fancy varieties available for sale as pets. ("Fancy" doesn't refer to a rat's appearance; it refers to domesticated rats bred to be owned as pets by rat "fanciers.") It is important to ask the pet shop manager where the shop's stock comes from; the stock's origins have a huge influence on your pet's social skills, health, and longevity.

A pet store can be a good source if the shop buys rodents from local breeders whose animals have been well cared for under good conditions. Other resources well worth investigating include local breeders, animal shelters, and your nearest fancy rat club. Although you will find a wealth of information and contacts online, it is important to exercise discernment—even a healthy skepticism—about purchasing animals sight unseen. Always try to meet with sellers and ask them questions about their practices.

Evaluating the Prospective Pet

No matter where you select your new pet, a few minutes of careful observation will help you choose a rat that will be both a good companion and easy to train. There are three main things to evaluate: the rat's environment and diet, the rat's health, and the rat's reaction to human contact.

Simply looking at the rat's environment will tell you a lot. Sellers who care about the welfare of their rats will keep their cages clean and provide some climbing apparatuses and toys. The food bowl will contain healthy foods such as lab cubes (also called lab blocks) or seed mixture, and the bedding will be soft, absorbent, and ink free. There will be little if any odor. Rats constantly groom themselves and one another. They don't like to live in filth. A dirty environment jeopardizes the animals' well-being and comfort; a clean environment promotes good health.

There are a few other things to look for in evaluating the health of the rat. First, make sure that no individual in that rodent colony is sneezing. Take a couple of minutes to listen to the rats. If you hear one sneeze, rule out the entire colony. Respiratory infections are highly contagious and often fatal—if one rat shows symptoms, you can be certain the infection has already spread. Don't waste your money.

Obesity can be a sign of overfeeding or a hormonal imbalance—in any case, be wary.

Second, in general, don't choose an overweight rat. Healthy rats fed a healthy diet are fairly active and normally do not get fat. A rat that is overweight and lethargic might be sick. There is one exception to this general advice. Rats surrendered to a local animal shelter or humane society for adoption are more often overweight than fit because their previous owners have not had time to interact with and stimulate them. You can still adopt these pudgy pals, though, and help them gradually get back into shape through exercise.

Always take some time to evaluate the social behavior of a rat that captures your interest. Rats are curious by nature and normally move around more once they're removed from a cage. Well-socialized rats are rarely still when taken to a new place or when being held by a new person. Try to engage the rat you're interested in with food or activity. Hold him for a while and see

With his dark head and striped back, the Hooded rat offers a striking alternative to the common Albino rat.

whether attention is all he needs to become more active and responsive. Hold him against your chest and listen closely for any wheezing sounds. These could be another sign of possible respiratory infection—in this case, move on.

Although rats are social creatures and prefer one another's company, it takes frequent handling by humans, starting at a very young age, to make them comfortable with their two-legged family members. You can generally gauge how much a rat has been handled by how it reacts when you reach into the cage and place your hand on the floor. A rat that runs in the opposite direction and hides in his house is a rat that wants nothing to do with humans. Perhaps he has been been picked up by his tail or otherwise handled roughly; perhaps he is merely unfamiliar with the presence of a big hand and wants nothing to do with it.

Proceed with caution: an unsocialized rat may bite, and that's the last thing you want your pet to do.

A rat that has been socialized from a very early age (picked up gently, spoken to, and cared for) will readily come to your hand, sniff at it, climb on it, and otherwise show interest in you. This is a winner. This rat won't run away every time you take him out. Instead, he will want to snuggle and play, learn tricks, and follow you around. And if he starts grooming you with gentle nibbles, take that as the ultimate compliment: this rat thinks you're one of his kind.

Choosing a Variety

Rats come in a variety of shapes, colors, and coat textures; the choice is up to you and your personal preferences. While most people are familiar with the Albino rat—the rat commonly used as a feeder for reptiles or in laboratories—most are unfamiliar with other types of Fancy rats, which come in a wide array of colors, including black, brown, gray, cream, and agouti (a ruddy brown ticked with black). There is also the Hooded rat, which has a colored head of black or beige and a stripe down the back.

Rats with the rarer varieties of coat include the Rex, which has curly hair, and the Satin, a rat with smooth, soft fur. If you want a unique structure, try the Tailless rat. There's also the Dumbo rat with, you guessed it, more elephantine ears.

Ever see a Siamese cat? Well, there are also "Siamese-colored" rats. These rats' heads and ears can range from chocolate to silver. Another rat variety whose name is borrowed from the cat world is the Russian Blue, a slate blue rat first seen in 1993.

There's even an Odd-Eyed rat with one red eye and one dark eye.

This Patchwork rat sports patches of fur that can change location from day to day.

Have allergies? Ever see the Mexican Hairless Dog and the Sphynx cat? These are relatively hairless breeds that can make life easier on humans with pet allergies. Rats, too, have been bred for hairlessness. This does not mean they have no hair at all. They do; it's just very fine and short. One variety of hairless rat is aptly named the Patchwork; its hair grows in differing patches from day to day. You never know how your Patchwork is going to look! Both the Hairless and Rex rats have crinkled whiskers and short hair on their faces. Hairless rats, like their canine and feline counterparts, need special consideration, as they are less able to adjust to shifts in temperature and easily catch cold.

If you are looking into rat ownership and you suffer from allergies, spend at least an hour with rats of various types prior to purchase. Some people with dog and cat allergies have no reaction to rats; others have more or less serious reactions to rats. It may be a contact irritation, rather than a true allergy, and may be easy to control with immediate washing after playtime. But it's always tough to give up a pet you love. Don't put yourself into a position of heartbreak. Test your reactions a few times, just to be sure.

Multiple or Single?

Rats are very social creatures. Wild rats live in colonies, and their domesticated relatives much prefer the company of other rats as well. A solitary rat will be lonely, move less, and have a shorter life span. I strongly suggest that you invite more than one rat into your life or consider adding a rat to the cage of an existing colony or another solitary rat that needs a companion.

These white domestic rats will keep each other company when their owner's at work.

There is very little additional work involved in owning multiple rats. The cage may need to be cleaned a day or two sooner, and they'll eat a little more, but Ben will be far happier having Ira in the picture than being alone.

Notice the use of two male names? Throughout this book I'll call our trainees Ben and Ira, or Sophie and Irma, to personalize the training process and to make an important point. Do consider owning more than one rat for your pet's well-being, but never obtain a male and female unless both are neutered. If you have an intact male and female, keep them separated. A rat can start breeding as early as five weeks of age, and a female can produce more than twelve pups per litter with a gestation of only

Make sure you keep males and females separated, or you will have more rats than you bargained for!

twenty-two days. As female rats go into heat cycles every four to five days, in a relatively short time she can breed again. In no time, you'll have a colony, not to mention a headache trying to find suitable homes for all those babies. So, keep Ben with Ira and Sophie with Irma. Decide on one sex, and stick to it. And while you're shopping, note whether the rats you observe are separated by sex; if not, and you choose an intact female, you're likely to get more than you bargained for—like twelve for the price of one!

Sex Choice

The sex you choose may depend on the activity level you desire. It also has some bearing on the overall appeal of the rat.

Female rats tend to be more delicately built and sleek. They're half the size of male rats and have little body oil or odor. Females also have a higher energy level than males do and tend to get into more mischief. Females investigate and nibble on everything. They also like to take things and hide them, as their nesting instinct is very strong. A female rat might need to get some play out of her system prior to any serious training. Because Sophie is so active, she might also have more endurance, and a higher tolerance of stressful situations, than Ben does.

Time to play? If you choose a high-energy female rat over a laid-back male, give her plenty of time to run about before training.

As youngsters, male rats have attention spans and energy levels equal to those of females, but as they age, males prefer to laze around more than climb and explore. As they age, male rats also tend to become smelly and their coats become greasy. One way to reduce the development of unpleasant odor is to neuter males. Neutering reduces not only the amount of care males require but also the male rat's tendency to become aggressive to both humans and other rats. A neutered male rat is happy to just sit on your lap watching television with you instead of crawling around in pockets and going on adventures. And he won't urine-mark!

Both males and females make good training candidates using the positive reinforcement methods detailed in this book. Keep in mind that a female rat may learn a tad faster and have a longer attention span, but she will need to be watched more closely when running free, as Sophie will be likely to run into things that aren't rat-friendly. Ben, by contrast, may learn a little more slowly but will be happy to nap on your lap far more than hunt hidden treasures, so if you're looking for a fellow couch potato, choose a male.

Remember to thoroughly research the traits and characteristics of the rats you are considering as pets before you make your final choice.

2

Rat-a-Roost

Before bringing your rat home for the first time, be sure everything—and everyone—is properly prepared for the newcomer.

Ben's homecoming should be preplanned. Rats are often an impulse purchase, but as you've picked up this book, I'm betting you want your relationship with Ben and Ira to last. Make the transition as comfortable and as stress free as possible, and you'll soon be ready to start training.

Part of your planning involves making sure you can afford the necessary supplies and equipment of rat ownership. Rats may not cost as much to own as other pets do, but you should be ready to dole out some funds for appropriate housing, vet care, and healthy food. It can cost upward of $300 per year to feed each rat and more than $100 for a good cage. The cost of bedding can also add up, especially if you buy commercial brands. Even routine veterinary checkups can run upward of $50 per year; caring for a rat with chronic health issues will cost much more, as many veterinarians consider rats exotic pets that require specialized services.

Regardless of your training intentions, by bringing Ben and Ira into your home you are taking them away from their family and friends. Granted, if you have purchased your rat at a pet shop, this probably happened before on some level. If you are adopting your rat at a shelter, it has probably adjusted to this trauma. But if you are obtaining your rat from a breeder, you can be certain that Ben and Ira have known no rats other than their families.

Rats quickly acclimate to new homes, but it should be done in a manner that minimizes undue stress and thus any resulting behavioral abnormalities or physical illness.

A wheel will provide your pets with hours of enjoyment, but avoid wire-runged models, as these could possibly lead to injury.

Are we there yet? Taking your new pet home in a soft carrier may not provide the security he needs—plus, remember those sharp teeth!

Coming Home

Before you take your rats home, consider their traveling arrangements. Dropping Ben into your pocket may be fine when he is in your home and already familiar with family, friends, and surroundings, but this is not a good idea on the first day. You can be certain that your rats will be anxious. Arrange travel conditions so that they add as little stress as possible—you'll be helping to make the adjustment to the new environment as smooth as can be.

Since Ben and Ira's homecoming will be a planned event, acquire and bring with you a proper, heavy-duty plastic or metal cage when you pick them up. Allowing the sales associate to place your rats in a small cardboard box is a bad idea. Rats chew, especially when stressed. Ben and Ira will chew their way right out of the box and have a free-for-all in your car in no time.

After all the excitement of moving, Ben may want to chill out for a while. Later, he will enjoy searching for hidden treasure in his blankets and sheets.

Your small travel cage should have comfortable bedding but no food or water, as this will only lead to wet messes. If you have an old piece of clothing such as a sweatshirt, cut off the sleeve and place this in the travel cage. This not only offers the rat a place to hide but also gets him used to your scent. Secure the cage in the backseat or enlist a passenger to hold the cage on his or her lap. Never drive with the rats on *your* lap.

The moment you arrive home, place Ben and Ira directly into their new, prepared abode, options for which are discussed in detail in chapter 3. There should be liberal offerings of food and water, clean bedding, and a hideaway where they can rest after all the commotion.

Acclimation to the Human Family

Allow Ben and Ira at least a day before you begin handling them and getting them used to you. Your rats need time to recover from the stress of leaving everything familiar, traveling to your house, and encountering the new digs. Children in the house will no doubt be excited to see the new pets and eager to hold the rats, but please don't allow this just yet. The commotion will further tax your animals, and they might bite from fear. Mostly, they'll just want to hide in a dark place until they settle in.

When a day or two has passed and everyone is relaxed, instruct children to pick up Ben and Ira and hold them gently but securely, without squeezing the poor creatures. Proper handling will help your rats adjust to their new family faster. Be certain to supervise all interactions between your rats and children.

Ben and Ira require close supervision around children and other house pets.

Acclimation to an Existing Colony

If Ben and Ira are your only rats, then it should be easy for them to adjust to their new surroundings. However, if your single rat is coming into a home where there is an existing colony, you'll need to make appropriate preparations, allowing Ira to establish himself without fear of fighting among the group.

Before you bring your new rat home, prepare two habitats: one for the main colony and one as a temporary home for your newcomer. As you most likely already have a temporary enclosure for cleaning days, simply clean both habitats thoroughly so that the colony's scent is subdued. Giving the colony cage a really good cleaning reduces any scent-marking, making the new cage a more welcome home for Ira.

Place the habitats close together on the same level. If you use aquariums, you need not worry about being too close. But if you have wire cages, make certain that the rats are close enough to see and smell each other but not close enough to touch noses.

When your rats no longer strain their noses through the cage or partake in staring contests, it is time to get them together. The best place for this is neutral territory, somewhere that does not carry the smell of any colony member. Many rat experts suggest a bathtub for this meeting, as it is free of rodent scent, has nothing that can injure the animals, and is easy to clean.

Getting your rats to "play nice" will require your patience and encouragement.

Bathtubs provide a safe, sanitary, scent-free neutral ground for rodent introductions.

Another way to make the meeting relatively stress free is to place a drop of vanilla flavoring on the top of each rat's head. This gives the rats the same scent, making it more difficult to discern who the newcomer might be. Remember to take these steps *very* slowly—rats can be quite pugnacious if they feel threatened!

Another great way to introduce your rats is to make them irresistible to each other. Take some vanilla or butterscotch pudding and smear a tiny dab on them. Then place them in the tub together. They'll be so busy licking and grooming both themselves and each other that they'll be friends in no time.

If you have several rats that need to meet a new rat, do so one at a time. Give each rat a chance to meet the new colony member alone. When all have met Ira, place two of the most accepting rats in with him. As they calm down and begin grooming each other, you can add a third colony member. Continue in this manner until the colony is one entity—there are no *outsiders*.

Once everyone is on a first-name basis, take the rats to their play area. This can be a tabletop or your lap. Be certain to keep a close eye on them. If any fighting occurs, separate the rats immediately and go back to square one with the individual cages and the entire bathtub scene. If everything goes well, they can all be returned to the main colony cage when playtime is over.

There may be a few scuffles at first as dominance is established within the colony. Rats instinctively establish dominance by forcing the newcomer to roll over and pinning him on his back for a few seconds. If Ira does not fuss, he'll be allowed to move away in short order. However, if he tries to fight back, you can expect some serious aggression and should not try to get the rats together so soon.

Initially, the pecking order is established through fairly frequent pushing around. The first encounters tend to be the worst, and they decrease in both intensity and frequency as Ira is accepted into the colony and learns his place within the hierarchy.

If you find that you have several male rats that tend to fight a lot, try neutering them. This often takes care of their aggression toward one another, but keep them separated for a couple of months, as it will take that long for the hormones to be eradicated from their systems.

Rat Nutrition

Rats are omnivores, like us: they eat both meat and vegetables. In the wild, they'll eat anything. This anything-goes diet is one reason why the rat is so successful in almost any environment. However, because rats have a barrier between their esophagus and stomach, they cannot vomit the way humans do after eating something toxic. Instead, rats' acute senses of smell and taste help them avoid poisonous substances; when they come across something new, they eat only a small amount until they establish

Rats like variety, but there are some items you should steer away from for health reasons, just as with people.

that it isn't poisonous. If it does induce unpleasant results, they quickly learn to identify and avoid it in the future. Keep this in mind when introducing Ben and Ira to new foods. Just because they don't gorge themselves right away doesn't mean they won't do so at a later time. They're just testing it first.

Most people buy whatever rat food they can find at a pet shop. While most rat food is fairly nutritious, it doesn't contain everything that Ben and Ira need in order to live long, healthy lives. The grains are processed, leaving fewer vitamins and minerals, and many products contain preservatives and food coloring to make them more appealing to us human buyers.

A little citrus may help boost your female rats' resistance to illness—but play it safe and toss the peel.

Lab blocks and seed diets contain too much corn, which can be both uncomfortable (as it can produce too much gas) and unhealthy as sole sources of nutrition. Debbie Ducommun, author of *Rats: Practical, Accurate Advice from the Expert*, suggests feeding your rat a diet consisting of 80 percent fortified commercial mix and 20 percent fresh fruits and vegetables.

On her Web site, www.ratfanclub.org, Ducommun also offers a recipe for a homemade rat diet. This includes fruit, vegetables (organic is always best), beef liver, oysters, sweet potatoes, cereal, molasses, and rice. These ingredients give the rat a well-rounded diet, much like it would consume in the wild. Receiving such good nutrition will possibly extend your rat's life and reduce the frequency of visits to the veterinarian for illnesses. Onesta Organics even makes a wonderful organic whole food supplement for rats (www.onestaorganics.com).

Be aware that some key foods will ward off illness or help your rat recover from a virus. For rats that have a family history of strokes, feeding celery, parsley, and prunes can reduce the incidence of this malady. Female rats can be fed oranges or orange juice, but these foods are not recommended for male rats, which can develop kidney damage or cancer from orange peel oil in the presence of a specific kidney protein. When trying to help your rat recover from a virus, or to boost resistance to viral infection, try feeding cranberries, strawberries, bananas, small amounts of garlic, raspberries, and mustard. How about a cup of green tea for that cold? Yes, rats benefit from a bit of tea as well.

Older rats, which may be prone to arthritis, can be fed cloves, ginger, garlic, and dates to help them maintain joint fluid and reduce inflammation. A sprinkle of whole-grain, vitamin-enriched breakfast cereal flakes is a source of antioxidants that help reduce cell damage and improve resistance to infection.

Rodents fed a diet that includes sunflower seeds often pick them out and leave the rest, which leads to an unbalanced, fattening diet.

Anything Doesn't Always Go

CERTAIN EVERYDAY FOODS ARE KNOWN TO HAVE HARMFUL, even fatal, effects on rats, so do your research on rat nutrition ahead of time. Debbie Ducommun warns about the following items on her Web site, www.ratfanclub.org:

- RAW DRY BEANS OR PEANUTS: These contain antinutrients—substances that interfere with the absorption or utilization of nutrients—and natural toxins that can destroy your rat's vitamin A and the enzymes needed to digest his food, namely the starches and proteins. This food can also cause a rat's red blood cells to clump.

- GREEN BANANAS: While ripe bananas have helpful healing properties, the green bananas inhibit starch-digesting enzymes. Make certain that you feed only yellow bananas.

- GREEN POTATO SKIN AND EYES: These contain solanine, which is a toxin.

- INSECTS: I advise against feeding rats anything other than grains, vegetables, and fruit. Exposure to nonregulated food items such as insects or discarded meats can sometimes be a health hazard, as they can contain parasites and carry disease.

- RAW BULK TOFU: Bulk tofu can contain bacteria that can be fatal to your rat. Buy only the packaged raw tofu, as it's been protected against bacteria.

You should also take care to limit the amount of nitrates in your rat's food. Too many cause a carcinogenic condition in the rat's stomach. Limit the amount of the following foods: corn (remember how common an ingredient this is in commercial diets?), eggplant, lettuce, radish, spinach, collard and turnip greens, beets, and celery. And, of course, no soda and candy bars. Rats may like them, but that doesn't mean you are being kind by offering them. Just as junk food causes obesity and health issues in humans, so it does in rats. Try the yogurt treats widely available in pet shops. These are far healthier than candies.

Another consideration is your rat's water. Tap water is normally chlorinated and fluorinated for human consumption. This is not good for your rat. In addition, if you live in an old home, your water may be traveling through old pipes made of lead, a mineral that can leach into the water with toxic effects. If you have well water, allow the water to run on cold for a minute or two before filling Ben and Ira's water bottle. This will allow any contaminants to wash out of the pipes before you offer the water to your rat. If you are unsure of your source, it doesn't hurt to give your rat distilled water, and it can be a great way to detoxify the system. Then you can be certain that your furry pet won't unknowingly be poisoned. Thoroughly cleaning Ben and Ira's water bottle every couple of days will also help reduce any mold and bacteria buildup.

Bedding

This is an important topic, since Ben and Ira will be spending their lives sleeping, exercising, and eating in their cages. They'll build nests with bedding material and often ingest particles of bedding as they nibble and play.

Sawdust is an option, but look for heat-treated and phenol- and dust-free varieties.

Give Ben and Ira some old, clean towels or blankets, but watch for stray threads, which can be harmful.

Most pet shops carry at least some of the more than a dozen bedding products suitable for small mammal cages. One popular choice, CareFresh, consists of short pulp fibers that look like shredded egg cartons. It is fluffy and soft and absorbs liquid pretty well, but it does not keep down odors. Another popular material, recyclable Eco-Bedding, looks like small, crinkled strips of brown paper. Some brands are made of Aspen bark or grain. Alfalfa pellets are another possibility but will likely be eaten by Ben and Ira, reducing their desire for more appropriate foods. You can use shredded paper from your shredding machine, but be certain that it contains no ink, which can be toxic to rats. Torn paper towels, tissues, or blank paper make great bedding but soil quickly, requiring more frequent cage cleaning.

Old clothing is a popular bedding but will need to be cleaned often and watched for stray threads. Ben and Ira can easily catch their feet on long threads and injure themselves. Be wary also of some of the shavings that are packaged as pet bedding. Cedar and pine shavings may contain a chemical, phenol, that might cause liver damage and respiratory illnesses in small mammals. Good pine-shaving products, such as Pet Pine and Feline Pine, have been kiln dried and offer great absorption as well as odor reduction.

While corncob bedding is becoming more popular for cat litter boxes, you might want to steer clear of this as a rat bedding. Rats are as likely to eat the material as to build a nest with it, and it's important to remember that too much corn is not healthy for your rodent.

For a detailed discussion of the pros and cons of all currently available rat beddings, I recommend the book *Training Your Pet Rat* by Gerry Bucsis and Barbara Somerville. Careful research of this issue will reduce the incidence of illness and death, giving you a healthy, happy rat. A happy rat will be more eager to learn and more capable of maintaining an attention span longer than two minutes. This will make training a much smoother process.

Veterinary Care

An essential part of preparing to bring a rat into your home is finding a veterinarian who works with rodents. Look for someone who specializes in small mammals. Check local yellow pages listings, and ask for references from local veterinary clinics. It may take some legwork to locate a veterinarian qualified to work on rats, especially outside big cities, as basic veterinary training

Rats need regular health care just as dogs and cats do. Look for a vet who specializes in small mammals.

focuses on more common pets, such as cats and dogs, or on large mammals such as horses. You want someone who not only takes a special interest in working with small mammals but also attends seminars and classes regularly to stay current on treating these pets. Two organizations that can be helpful in locating a qualified veterinarian are the Rat Fan Club (www.ratfanclub.org) and the Rat and Mouse Club of America (www.rmca.org).

The first visit to your vet should take place shortly after you acquire your rat. Your vet will perform a general examination, check Ben's eyes and ears, palpate the abdomen, and listen to the heart and lungs. You will be asked where you purchased your rat, what you're feeding, and what kind of bedding you use. If you have any questions about proper care and equipment, a qualified rodent vet should be able to answer them.

Next, you should consider scheduling neutering or spaying your rats between three and six months of age—sooner rather than later for a female, since she may be ready to breed by the age of five weeks. Spaying and neutering has many health and behavioral benefits beyond population control. For Sophie, it can mean prevention of both mammary and pituitary tumors, which are caused by hormonal changes when ovulation stops. In other words, it's a side effect of rat menopause. Mammary tumors, common in females, are often benign but still require surgery, causing undue stress on Sophie's body. A pituitary tumor is often fatal. Symptoms can range from lethargy to loss of coordination and paralysis.

A male rat should be neutered between three and four months of age to achieve the most beneficial results. These include a less oily coat, less territorial marking, a lower incidence of aggressive behavior, a reduced chance of hormone-related cancers associated with age, and lowered risk of prostate disease and kidney degeneration.

If you want your rat to live a long and healthy life, give it the medical care it needs. For further advice, see Debbie Ducommun's *Rats*, which describes many of the diseases and infections common in these animals, how to recognize them, and in many cases, how to deal with them.

3

Rat Domain

A small plastic carrier such as this should be used for transportation and not as a permanent home.

Part of the fun of rat ownership is watching Ben and Ira cavort in their cages. It's no fun to watch a rat simply lie there, unmoving, sleeping. It's no fun for the rat, either. Rats prefer activity. They love to move around, socialize, and exercise. That's just what they'll do if you provide a stimulating environment for Ben and Ira. This includes rodent company. No rat should live by itself. Rats prefer to live in colonies, and isolation leads to intense loneliness.

Condo, Townhome, or Single Family

We all have our preferences when it comes to how much house we want or how much yard we want to care for. The larger the size of the property, the more work involved in maintaining it.

Rats are curious and tend to be more active if allowed out of their cages—just be sure to supervise them.

Keep this in mind when deciding how many rats you want to own and how you will house them. Consider house and grounds, both of which will become horribly stinky and pest ridden if they are not kept very clean.

You have many housing options. The two most popular choices are wire cages and aquariums. On occasion, you can also find appropriate Plexiglas containers. Not just any wire cage, aquarium, or Plexiglas container will do, however. You must ensure proper airflow, maintain sanitary conditions, and consider safety factors.

Containers to avoid are made of plastic (including gerbil, hamster, or chinchilla habitats), wood, and metal that is not coated. Keeping rats in these containers is dangerous for several reasons. First, rats chew. They chew wood, plastic, and anything else they can get their teeth on. They can easily chew their way through a cage that might otherwise hold a hamster or a bird.

Rats love hiding in little cubbies such as this one; however, those made of cloth aren't safe as long-term playhouses since they're so easily chewed apart.

Housing your rat in an uncoated metal cage poses sanitation issues and the possible problem of rust ingestion, which can kill a rat. Treated woods contain toxic preservatives that give off gases, also endangering the health of your rat.

If you're looking for an easy-care environment and intend to own only one or two rats, a 10- to 20-gallon aquarium works pretty well, provided you keep the top screened to allow ventilation and never place the aquarium in direct sunlight. An aquarium allows your rats to see the world and remain safe. It also keeps the litter within the aquarium, making the entire room less stinky and dirty. With a house, a wheel, chewies, toys, and a water bottle, Ben and Ira have it made.

A Plexiglas cage is very similar to an aquarium. Some Plexiglas containers have small ventilation holes perforating the upper walls; some merely rely on a screened top to allow airflow. Either way, there's no litter mess, all odors are more or less contained, and your rats are safe.

Wire cages come in a range of sizes and designs, primarily single-level square cages, two-level upright cages, and three-level

Bumblefoot

A BACTERIAL INFECTION IN THE HEEL, BUMBLEFOOT IS *typically associated with genetic factors or an unsanitary living environment (e.g., old, soiled litter). The infection manifests as a round red swelling ("bumble") or lesion on the bottom of the foot that eventually erupts in a yellowish scab. Although bumblefoot is not necessarily linked with wire-floor cages, the wires can place unneeded pressure on the feet and could exacerbate the problem. Prevention is the best cure here: eliminate potential sources of the malady by replacing or covering wire floors with plastic mats and cleaning your rat's cage regularly. Topical antiseptics, in addition to oral or injected antibiotics, may combat the infection, which if left untreated could be fatal, but many can actually inhibit healing. Avoid overusing Betadine, hydrogen peroxide, or ChlorhexiDerm; usually, diluting these with saline in the early stages of injury is OK. Wound dressings over the ulcers are also a big help. In addition, pain medication may be available from your vet.*

ferret cages. Any of these will work, provided the wire is spaced close enough to prevent escape or getting one of the rat's feet caught within the grid. It is highly recommended that you have a solid floor for the bedding, as rats can injure their feet by constantly having to walk on a wire grid and cannot make a comfortable bed if their bedding is constantly slipping through the wire into a pan below.

A single-family home might be great for the single rat or maybe even two rats, but a multilevel cage is far healthier, because the larger the environment is, the more exercise the rats can get without your having to take them out of their cages. So if you must meet a tight work or school schedule, make sure Ben and Ira have a large enough and stimulating enough environment to move around in. If you plan on spending loads of time with your rat and allowing him to run in his ball or walk with you on a leash, you don't need to keep him in a large home, just a comfortable one.

If you want to own more than two rats, opt for the ferret cage, as it has two or three levels with ramps and coated wire that is easy to clean. The wire mesh also makes for great climbing adventures, as rats can grip the grids with their dextrous feet. Anyone for hanging upside down?

Another great thing about a wire-grid cage is that you can hang hammocks from the tops of the various levels. Rats love to sleep in hammocks. There are even enclosed hammocks in which your rat can feel totally secure.

Many items available for large birds are also great for rat environments: toys, perches, climbing apparatuses, and chewies. Because many of these items are fashioned with hooks or clips, attaching them to a wire-grid cage is easy, and they are easy to clean and remove.

Enriching the Rodent Environment

To have a more interactive pet rat, you will need to offer him a stimulating environment, one filled with things to do and places to go. The more options there are, the more entertaining Ben and Ira will be for you to play with and watch.

While there are many cage options, in my opinion, there's only one you should consider for the most enriching environment: the multiple-level cage. Multiple-level models are readily available at large pet shops or from Internet retailers. Do a little research on the Web, and you're sure to find something suitable.

Within the cage, you should have tunnels, houses, a tree branch, and a rodent wheel large enough to accommodate the largest of your rat pals. Bird toys and perches often make great rat paraphernalia, as the sandpaper-like finishes of the perches help keep your rat's claws trim. Be sure to give your rat toys that he can safely both chew on and climb around.

Bird playgrounds also make great rat playgrounds. Rats love climbing ladders and running along narrow ledges, hanging off platforms and hiding in treehouses. Once Ben and Ira acclimate to this play area, you can train them to go over any number of obstacles on cue.

Another great play and exercise item is the plastic ball. Placed inside this large see-through ball, your rat can travel wherever he wants to go. I've found it's a great way to safely exercise the rat and protect the furniture. Just watch out for stairs. The ball can also be used in training your rat to come when called or to follow you around inside or out.

If you really want to have some fun, invest in or make a play yard that has a ladder, climbing rope, platforms, tunnels, and hidey-holes. You really needn't do anything to get Ben and Ira used to

Rats should have plenty of toys to keep their nimble brains busy.

these objects other than to place some of their food throughout the play environment. This creates a great game of hide-and-seek, simulating what your rats would do in the wild: searching out food and shelter. It's fun to watch them gallivant around, and you'll have the satisfaction of knowing you are increasing Ben's and Ira's curiosity, memory, and reasoning abilities.

Rats are naturally curious and will investigate small, dark places and climb any surface that feels secure enough to hold them. Enabling Ben and Ira to investigate will fulfill this need as well as give them loads of exercise.

Your pet rat can quickly learn a pattern. Hide a morsel of food somewhere twice, and he'll be looking in that spot for a long

Above, a rat prepares to enter a large plastic ball for some fun and exercise. Below, another active rat clambers through a ring.

time. Researchers studying pattern recognition, memory, and problem solving learned long ago that rats make excellent experimental subjects because they perform so well in mazes. Observing a rat confronted with a mystery is loads of fun for you, too, as they work their way around the problem or solve a puzzle.

In fact, the methods described in this book originated with studies in rat maze behavior. Various "problems" were created to observe how a rat solved them or overcame negative experiences to complete the maze pattern and receive the food reward. Did the rat learn? Or did he merely react in the moment? The experimental psychologists performing the study discovered that rats do learn and do memorize patterns. You can emulate these studies just for the fun of it. Which of your rats learns faster? Which one has a better memory? Wouldn't this be a great project for a science fair? There are many places you can go with these ideas. Keep an open mind, and always ensure Ben and Ira's safety.

This play yard is designed for birds, but it's perfect for rats, too.

Exercise Options

You already know about the plastic ball, but what about just allowing Ben and Ira to race around your house? Not a good idea. There are so many ways in which this risks injuring the rat as well as damaging your home and possessions. Remember how much rats like to chew? What if they chew up an electrical wire? That can be extremely dangerous.

Rats seek small, dark places for safety. What happens when you can't find your pet rat? He may run loose for an extended period of time or escape outdoors, where any number of dangers await.

Scampering up and down his ladder, this rat gets lots of good exercise.

Rats adore a good tunnel—you can find all sorts of options in stores or make your own.

Never leave your rat loose in your home. You are far better off either letting your rat roll around in the enclosed ball or teaching him to walk on a leash. And always keep in mind the multilevel home and a companion or two for play.

Human and rodent roommates enjoy some playtime together. Remember to supervise interactions between your children and new pets.

4

Rat Manner

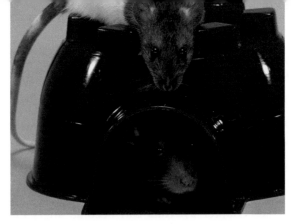

To train your rats, you first need to learn all about them. For instance, rats feel secure in small, tight places.

Understanding the nature, typical behaviors, and likes and dislikes of rats is essential if you wish to properly care for and train them. First and foremost, you need to know about their social organization.

One reason why rats are particularly good research-study subjects is that their social organization is similar to the social organization of humans. Rats form family and community (colony) groups with a clear social order. Each colony has a governor; each "household," a family director. In general, rat society functions smoothly as long as no individual tries to change his position in the social hierarchy. When individuals challenge the director, scuffles and fights break out that tend to upset the entire colony.

One research study involving rats tested the relationship between overpopulation and aggression. The more crowded the environment, the more aggressive the rats became. So if you plan to have a rat colony of more than two individuals, make certain that the cage can house its residents without overcrowding. In addition, make sure that all residents are introduced on neutral territory (see chapter 2). Rats can become angry enough to inflict horrific, even fatal, wounds on one another.

Learning to live harmoniously has much to do with education. The higher the education, the easier it will be to get along. The more you stimulate Ben and Ira, the happier they will be and the better they will behave toward each other. Each rat needs equal attention. Take the time to work with both (or all three, four, or more) daily.

Rats are by nature nocturnal creatures. Left to themselves, they will perform all of their antics at night. So if you have a

Two cozy rats from the same colony present a united front to observers. Rats are social creatures, with many of the same traits as humans.

squeaky wheel in their enclosure, either take it out prior to bedtime or place their cage in a soundproof room. You can be certain that the wheel will be turning, and squeaking, a good part of the night. That's not likely to strengthen the bond between you and your rat.

When you begin training, you will be changing Ben and Ira's nocturnal schedule quite a bit, as they'll be receiving all sorts of activity and food during the day. You may soon have a good night's sleep. As rats are very adaptable to their surroundings, your little guys will quickly learn to adjust to your schedule.

Grooming Behavior

Rats love to groom themselves and one another. It's a form of socializing—compare it to girls' doing one another's hair and nails at a slumber party. As rats prefer to be clean, they will spend lots of time licking one another and nibbling off dry flakes of skin. On occasion, you can observe one rat holding down another to be groomed. This actually has two purposes: to hold the groomee still and to tell that groomee that the groomer is the boss. It's a means of expressing dominance.

Petting your rat is in effect grooming him. Many rats will hold their heads down as they are being groomed. However, they won't maintain this posture for long, as they would much rather explore than remain in one spot.

Your rat will invite grooming by lying still with his head down. Some rats enjoy your touch and the grooming process so much that their eyes will appear to bulge in and out, and you might hear their teeth grinding. "Oh, that's nice," says Ben. "Just a little behind the ears," says Ira. Should your rat roll onto his back for a tummy rub, you're a real rat charmer!

Rats will sometimes groom their owners—take it as a compliment!

Many rats bond with their people enough to groom them, too. The animals will lick and sometimes nibble a bit to take off skin flakes. While this habit might be a little scary at first, it rarely hurts, as the nibbles are very shallow, more like tickles. If Ira does get a little carried away with those nibbles, squeak and pull away. Ira will understand that the grooming became too serious and back off a bit.

Rat Bites

It is indeed rare for a domesticated rat to bite without reason. Fancy rat varieties really aren't aggressive animals. Contrary to historical popular opinion, rats prefer to be social and affection-ate. If you are bitten by your rat, there is a reason. Identify the reason and learn what to do, and what not to do, to avoid repeat-ing the incident.

Warn other people not to poke their fingers in your rats' cage—unless they want those fingers bitten.

Rats will bite when frightened, startled, or in pain or to protect their territory. Many rats can be wary of strangers, especially if they haven't been properly socialized as pups. If a stranger reaches into the cage or pokes a finger through the bars, there is a good chance he or she will be bitten. Rats also bite at their food; if you give Ben food every time you visit with him, he'll learn to associate your extended hand with food and bite at your fingers, expecting food to be there.

The more you handle Ben and Ira, the more acclimated they'll be to you and others. Try to spend at least a half hour to an hour per day training, playing with, and cuddling Ben and Ira. Rats enjoy this interaction, even if they do have the company of other rats.

Activity

Rats, especially females, instinctively move around. They are very curious and love to search out dark places. Their keen sense

Bite Prevention

Use soap and water before and after handling your rat.

HERE ARE A FEW SUGGESTIONS TO KEEP YOURSELF AND OTHERS FROM BEING BITTEN:

1. *When you play with your rat, make sure that you first wash your hands thoroughly so that there is no scent of food on your fingers. This is also a sensible practice if you are handling several different rat colonies within a short time period, as you can pass a bacterial infection from one colony to another.*

2. *Never tease Ben and Ira. If feeding by hand, hold the food still. Otherwise, as they try to reach for the food, they'll become frustrated and use their teeth instead of their paws.*

3. *Never startle your rats by grabbing them. Always give them a chance to crawl onto your hand to be lifted for playtime, training, or cuddling.*

4. *Use consistent signals at all times. When you are ready to begin a training session, tap the surface with your target stick (see chapter 5). When you wish to offer playtime, either insert a ladder into the play area or hold your hand flat on the surface and allow Ben and Ira to climb aboard.*

5. If Irma has babies, let her decide whether she wants to socialize with you or not. Some mommy rats become very protective of their babies. It would be best to place a ladder into the play area in the cage and allow Irma to come out if she wishes. When she comes out, then you can offer your hand for social time.

6. Make sure that visitors to your home do not stick their fingers or food through cage openings. This is both frightening and frustrating for rats as they try to take food from unfamiliar hands and find that their paws can't quite reach it. Chances are they'll try using teeth.

7. Allow new or frightened rats an adjustment period. Don't forget that a frightened rat will bite. This can take anywhere from a few hours to a couple of days. You'll know when your rat is moving around, curious, instead of trying to hide in dark places. A curious rat is content. Time to play.

8. If your rat is injured and you must handle him in order to treat or transport him, wrap the rat in a towel. Not only will this insulate you from feeling his teeth, but it will also offer more security for your rat, reducing the chance that you'll be bitten.

Let your rat adjust to his surroundings before handling; he will feel less overwhelmed and threatened.

of smell is also a driving factor, and they can locate tiny particles of food at great distances. Their long whiskers help them move around in small, dark places, because they translate the terrain as the animals move through it, much as the whiskers on felines, who also tend to be nocturnal, do.

A rat will seek some sort of solid vertical surface along which to move. Hence, you'll see your rats run along a wall or the sides of furniture as they explore. This gives the rodent a sense of stability as well as added security, since they can't be attacked from all sides.

Chewing and Tearing

Rats chew. There's no getting away from it. It's what they do. It's how they spend their time. It's how they build their nests. It's how they play. If a substance isn't made of metal, a rat can chew it.

When you have your rat out and about, you'll need to keep a close eye on what objects go into his mouth. Everything is fair game, from your clothing to the couch you sit on. It's best to prepare the rat's play area prior to allowing him free rein, and it's up

If you let your rat out of his cage, you may wish to hide any chewables you don't want damaged.

Make sure that every item in your rat's cage will survive his chewing and tearing.

to you to provide safe chew toys. Place an old sheet or clothing over surfaces you want to protect so that you won't be upset when it is riddled with holes. Better the old sheet than the expensive couch cushions.

Paper is a favorite rat toy. Rats will spend hours shredding and packing the pieces into bedding. You must be certain that all paper within reach of Ben and Ira is clear of potentially toxic substances such as inks.

Plastic will also fall victim to Ben and Ira's chewing frenzies. Never use plastic in their cages. Any dishes, cage clips, water bottles, or trays made of it will be destroyed sooner or later. You'll be far better off using stainless steel dishes in a metal cage with metal housings. Your rats will put their teeth on the metal but not be able to chew it to pieces.

As you want to stimulate your rats by putting toys, ladders, and ropes in their cage, you must accept the fact that these will need to be replaced every so often. Ditto for sleeping hammocks.

Ropes are great for climbing but are not safe for chewing—supervise carefully.

If you feel your pet shop's rodent aisle is lacking, check out the bird toys!

Rats love sleeping hammocks, but some will chew the straps that keep the hammocks anchored to the top of the cage.

Many kinds of safe rat chew toys are available in pet shops and online. You can also select chew toys from the many colorful toys sold for exotic birds. The great thing about bird cage toys is they can hang from the top of a cage, giving your rat something to climb on as well as a safe chew toy.

Dog chew toys are another possibility. Not only are these healthy chew toys, but they also help keep Ben and Ira's teeth ground to healthy lengths. Nylabones, Booda Velvets, Gourmet Health Chews, and even regular dog biscuits are good choices. The rope toys can be suspended from different areas of the cage, offering a virtual jungle gym for Ben and Ira. The options for their home and playground are enormous. Let your imagination take you on a rat adventure!

5

Rat-a-Tat, Tap

For added ease in training, sessions should begin at mealtime.

Now we've reached the heart of this book: rat training. You're well versed in essential rat care and have taken the necessary steps to ensure that Ben and Ira are healthy, happy, and ready to learn. Remember that a stressed or ill rat is unable to tolerate any level of strain, even if it is a fun educational game.

To successfully train your Ben or Ira, you will need to use the daily feeding sessions as training sessions. While some rats may eventually perform for the reward of freedom or play, they rarely work for human praise. Few, if any, will initially work for play. You will need to rely on a fail-safe motivator. Food will do it every time.

Reward-based learning is a positive means of developing fast responses, creating an enjoyable environment in which your rat is willing to interact, eager to learn, and happy to spend time with

Placing treats in the training area quickly acclimates your student to the space.

you. Ben and Ira will have something to look forward to each day. A working rat is healthier, both mentally and physically.

Prepare for training by deciding what type of food reward you will use. The choice is up to you: Ben's regular cubes, fresh vegetables, or yogurt treats. You don't have to use the same food every training session. In fact, the more you vary the reward, the more your rat will remain interested in obtaining it.

I've always done a quick morning training session by having my rats come when called and rise up on their hind legs to receive their food cube. One each is all they need. Sometimes I vary the routine by having them traverse obstacles along the way, such as an A-frame, jumps, and tunnels. Rat agility!

In the evenings, my rats earn their yogurt treats by following me in their exercise ball or learning new tricks. Often, I just place the treats throughout their exercise areas so that they get to have treasure hunts. This simulates natural environments and gives them loads of exercise as well.

If you have been free feeding Ben to this point (allowing him unlimited access to food), you might need to either use a very high-value reward or food deprive him for twelve to twenty-four hours prior to initiating the training. Usually, using a high-value food is sufficient, but some rats can be very finicky and prefer their cubes or seeds so much that it is difficult to substitute anything not part of their normal diet as a reward. You may not discover this until you begin the training process. Lackluster responses will be most pronounced in an overweight rat rescued from a shelter. This rat was obviously free fed for a long time, and his obesity makes him very lethargic. It might take a while for him to decide to move around a bit to eat.

The tapping finger signals that food is available.

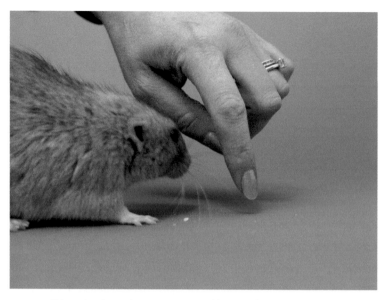

This rat has learned to come to a tap without needing to receive food.

Creating the Learning Environment

You can begin by working Ben and Ira in their cage or on an uncluttered table in a quiet room. The less distraction, the better, as you need your rat to concentrate on learning, not playing or eating something other than a treat that was earned. If you are going to be using apparatuses such as tunnels, hoops, and stools, allow Ben and Ira to explore the structures for a while prior to the training session. However, don't start working with an apparatus until your rat understands some basics such as *come* and *follow*.

The surface of the training area should be nonslippery and easy to clean. Rats rarely contain their waste and will relieve themselves wherever they happen to be. An easy-to-clean surface will allow you to train Ben and Ira with little interruption as you quickly wipe off the waste.

Rats may be frightened by unfamiliar people but are rarely fearful of new objects. If you find that your rat shows any hesitation nearing an object used in training, however, put a morsel of food on it. Once Ben associates an object with food, he will be back for more. Rats never forget where food can be found. They may be rodents, but they have superior intelligence, pattern memory, and adaptability; that is why they are such a successful species all over the world.

Noting that rats have excellent pattern memory brings me to the next point: vary the training exercises so that you are teaching Ben and Ira to respond to your cues, not to a specific pattern. If you use an apparatus, move it around from training session to training session. When teaching your rat to come to you, don't always stand or sit in the same place. Move to different areas. This will aid in the development of your pet rat's brain instead of merely teaching a pattern. Any rodent can do a maze. An exceptional rodent actually understands how to communicate with and respond to you, process new patterns, and solve new problems.

If you plan to conduct training sessions in a specific area, begin using this area for feeding times. Before you know it, Ben and Ira will be running from their cages directly to the training area, ready to go.

Training Preparation

You must lead your rat into an appropriate response. Therefore, you must be able to let Ben and Ira know the moment they are performing correctly. What happens when you see your rat doing something right but can't get the words out in time? By the time Ben and Ira move, it's too late. Timing of a reward is crucial. The

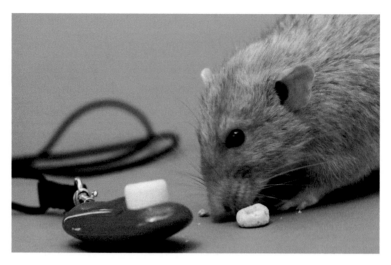

A clicker instantly marks the moment your rat performs as you wish.

behavior expressed at the moment you reward is the behavior that will be repeated.

Use of Positive Reinforcement Training Markers

Once you have chosen the ideal training treat and training location, you're ready to teach Ben and Ira the meaning of a reinforcing marker. Rats are some of the first creatures ever tested to respond to positive reinforcement training markers. The marker can be any specific sound paired with a reward. The easiest tool for this is a clicker.

A clicker is a small plastic box with a metal tongue that, when depressed and released, makes a clicking sound. Each clicker produces a distinct sound. This tool can be easily operated with your thumb and a couple of fingers to stabilize it, leaving your other hand free to lure and cue your rat during training.

When you are training, I suggest that you reward Ben with tiny morsels or he will quickly fill up and no longer have an interest in training. Another drawback to using large morsels is that your rat will spend a lot of time eating, taking away from your precious training time allotments. (Few of us can spend the entire day training our rats.)

As most animals learn best when they know what to expect, be consistent. Present a new idea in a simple manner. The moment Ben and Ira respond, click and reward. Again, timing is crucial. An animal only acknowledges a correct action when you mark the moment of that action. That's why using a clicker is useful, as it is far easier, simpler, and faster to press your thumb than to form words or tap a finger on a hard surface. Keep in mind that rats don't care as much about your voice as a dog or

Pair the sound of the clicker with the giving of a treat to get your point across. The clicker, shown here only for illustration, should be out of rat sight.

cat might. But they do recognize specific sounds that bring rewards or result in something negative.

Do not hold the clicker near your rat or point it at him like a television remote control. Ira's hearing is actually quite good and he'll be wondering what you're offering if you point the clicker at him. Is it another toy? Maybe food? Keep the clicker either at your side or behind your back. There's no need for your rat to see where the noise originates.

Condition your rat to the clicker in the following manner:

1. Show your rat the treat.
2. When your rat sniffs at the food, click and allow him to eat the food.
3. Repeat at least five times.

Your pet rat is sure to identify the clicking sound with the dispensing of food within a very short time. You'll know for sure when you see his little whiskers and nose quivering as he requests more food.

Teach your rat to target on your hand by placing some food on a finger—but be careful.

Baby food smeared on the target stick expedites teaching your rat to target.

Now you can start luring him with the food.

1. Allow your rat to sniff the food, but don't give it to him.
2. Move it slightly to one side.
3. When your rat moves his head toward the food morsel, click and give him the food.

Repeat the luring sequence in all directions. Up, down, left, and right. Don't make Ben or Ira do more than move their heads to look at the food. This is a very important first step, and you don't want to cause any anxiety about chasing after food morsels. Teach your rats that they merely have to follow the direction of the food to earn it.

This step will further reinforce the clicking sound with the delivery of a reward.

After only a couple training sessions, Ben and Ira will have a complete understanding of the meaning of the click.

Use of Cues as Reinforcers

As you lure Ben and Ira into any number of new behaviors, you are using specific visual cues with each action. Your rat is learning that following these movements will be very rewarding. Thus, your pet rat is being reinforced—rewarded—by following the cues.

It is a good idea to write down all of the different tricks and behaviors you will be teaching your rat. Each behavior will need to be paired with a specific cue in order for the cue to remain a clear communicator. I recommend the use of hand gestures, a target stick, or both.

A target stick should have some means of holding a food morsel on the end. You can make a simple target stick by taping a small spoon or fork to a quarter-inch-diameter dowel or an old wooden spoon. For overzealous rats who love their lab cubes, a pair of tongs works very well, as you can cue and reward without the risk of getting scraped by a tooth. Along the way, you'll be able to teach your

Hold the target stick near your rat's head so he looks upward.

rat how to use his forepaws instead of his teeth to take the food. This will make the reward process far less stressful, as most people tend to hesitate or unconsciously pull away after receiving a rat bite, no matter how accidental. Rats generally only bite when angered or frightened, and this rarely occurs during a positive training experience. But as the saying goes, once bitten, twice shy; this will make the training process less enjoyable, so you might want to take precautions.

There are two main cues that can branch off into more complex behaviors: the tap and the lure. The tap cues the rat to come to you. The lure can teach Ben and Ira to go over, onto, and through obstacles; turn in any direction; or touch an object.

The tapping cue is one of the best reinforcers, as your rat learns that coming to you brings food and attention rewards. Thus, you'll get a terrifically positive response to the tap.

Once Ben and Ira understand that the presence of the target stick means that food can be easily obtained, it too becomes a positive cue.

THE COME-TO-A-TAP

The best first behavior you teach your rat is to come to you when you call. As he doesn't yet understand your words, you cannot rely on the come command to have any meaning.

If you have already worked on the clicker preparations, Ben and Ira will understand moving toward a food morsel and receiving the reward. The come exercise is merely an extension of the head movement-reward game.

1. Show your rat the food morsel.
2. When he shows interest by sniffing in the direction of the food, click and reward.

3. Repeat this two more times.

4. Place the food a couple of feet away, and tap the surface of the table next to the food.

5. When your rat comes toward the food, click and allow the rat to get his reward.

6. Repeat this by waiting slightly longer prior to clicking. For example, you placed the food morsel 2 feet from Ben. The previous time, you clicked when he began going to the food; this time, wait until he's gone at least halfway. You know that he'll go all the way, but he doesn't yet know the full meaning of the tap. However, he does know that the clicker means the rewards are coming. Thus, when you tap the table surface, in effect giving him a cue that carries rewards, Ben will quickly understand the meaning.

7. The next time you tap the surface, click when your rat reaches the food morsel, and allow him to eat his reward.

Now Ben and Ira understand that your tap means they will be rewarded for coming. You can use this basic response for almost anything from traversing apparatuses to following you while in the plastic exercise ball. The come-to-a-tap is the basis for all other rodent work.

LURING

When training with a lure, it is best to use a high-value reward such as a yogurt treat, pieces of fruit, or cheese, all foods that are certain to grab your rat by the taste buds. An attentive rat is one that can be lured over and through anything. This means of controlling direction has unlimited possibilities.

The rat will soon associate the target stick with rewards.

Let's first teach Ben and Ira how to follow the lure.

1. Place the target stick on the table surface. Put a high-value treat on the business end of the stick.
2. Tap your finger next to the food on the target stick.
3. Click and reward when your rat arrives.
4. Repeat this at least five times, moving the target stick to different places on the table.

To be certain that Ben and Ira have a good idea of what it means to go to the target stick, touch it, and get a click with reward, proceed with the following test:

1. Place the target stick, without a treat, on the table surface.

*T*EACH YOUR RAT TO GO INSIDE THE PLASTIC BALL

1. *Place the ball in a secure location where it cannot roll around if your rat should place his foot on it.*
2. *Put a piece of food in the ball.*
3. *Place your rat nearby so that he can smell the food.*
4. *When your rat enters the ball, click with your clicker, and allow the rat to eat the food morsel.*
5. *Let your rat exit on his own. After he exits, repeat steps one through four.*

Within a short time Ben and Ira will be going into the ball to see if it holds treats.

The next phase of this exercise is to have your rat enter the ball without being lured by the treats. As Ben and Ira have learned that the ball contains food, there will be a very quick response as they will eagerly enter the ball as soon as it's presented.

1. *Place the ball in the same nonrolling position as before.*
2. *Allow your rat to approach.*
3. *When your rat enters the ball, click and give the rat a reward after he is inside.*
4. *Repeat this a few times until it is well learned.*

Now we add the ball movement. Up to now we made sure that the ball was secure and nonmoving. However, if you want your rat to go into the ball when you aren't holding it, he must accept the fact that it will move around when he presses against the edge.

The behavior markers are the same as with the previous exercises, but I suggest you start with the first exercise of baiting Ben and Ira into the ball, as the rats must have great incentive to enter a moving room. Once they are comfortable with this, you will find they'll walk right on in of their own accord and await their marker and reward.

This process can take anywhere from one training session to a week of training sessions. Resist the temptation to force your rat into this closed-in environment as he'll immediately want to leave instead of learn why you want him inside. Rats work far more efficiently if they believe their behavior is voluntary.

Once you have Ben and Ira acclimated to the rolling plastic ball, close the top. Do so only briefly. After a couple of seconds, click, open the top, and give your rat a reward. Gradually increase the amount of time you keep the ball closed. This will acclimate your pet rat to remaining inside without causing panic.

Placing food around the entrance to the ball will quickly teach your rat that the ball's a fun place to be.

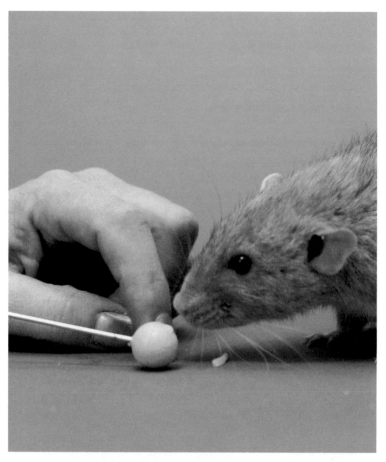

Tapping next to the food and target stick teaches the rat that the stick is also a food dispenser.

2. Tap the surface at the target end of the stick.

3. When your rat arrives, click, but make him wait very briefly for the reward to come from somewhere other than the end of the stick. Don't make him wait too long or his desire to come to the tap will be extinguished. The reward must be delivered very quickly at this point. Drop the reward at the tip of the stick; don't hand-feed.

As you repeat this exercise, moving the target to different locations, gradually increase the time between the click and the delivery of the reward. As rats live in the moment, increase this time in increments of mere seconds, not minutes. A second is an hour to a rat. Luckily, they have such enormous food drives that they usually keep doing whatever it was that delivered the food until the food is again given. This makes them very forgiving of a trainer's poor timing.

Another problem with waiting too long is that Ben and Ira might just think the target stick is supposed to be the edible reward and start nibbling on it. You don't wish to establish this behavior, as the stick is a cue, not a reward.

One of the great advantages of training with a target stick is that you can lure your rat to areas above or otherwise beyond your own reach. You can tap the stick on any surface to get Ben's and Ira's attention. And using a stick that is narrower than a finger allows you to insert it into tight spaces you could not squeeze a finger into. This translates to a wider variety of activities for Ben and Ira. Best of all, the rats don't get the wrong impression that the food comes from your fingers, reducing the potential for "biting the hand that feeds."

6

Rat on a Rope

Always allow your rat to sniff new things, especially the body harness you will be using to walk him.

REALISTICALLY, WHAT CAN YOU EXPECT FROM BEN AND Ira? What is the rat attention span? How long can they work? How much can they learn?

Rats are one of the most successful species on earth. They thrive in virtually any environment. What does this tell you about their learning abilities? Everything! An animal that learns quickly is more likely to adapt quickly. Look at the human race. We learn how to use our environment to our best advantage.

Successful training depends both on your rat's natural learning abilities and on your own time commitment and imagination. As with any new activity, begin slowly. Break each behavior down into smaller, easily achievable steps, and build one step on another until the final goal is reached. But why stop at one goal when there are so many others ahead? When we climb stairs, are we happy we made it up one riser? Or do we continue to the top?

You have chosen to own and train a rat. Rats aren't dogs. They don't have the same loyalties. But they can learn as much as any canine can. The sky's the limit with Ben and Ira.

Leash Training

Some of the basic behaviors dog owners teach their pets are to come when called, walk with them, sit, lie down, and stay. Walking obediently on a leash is fundamental, as nearly every populated area has canine leash laws. While some dogs are small enough to be comfortably carried, most are not and must be trained to accept a leash, for their own safety as well as the safety of others.

As a rat owner, you're very lucky; you can put your small companion in a pocket. But consider being more adventurous by training your rat on a leash. Leash training allows your rat to interact with the natural world beyond his cage and your home. The more variety there is in Ben and Ira's environment, the more stimulated and curious they become. Moreover, a leash-trained rat gets more exercise, making him far healthier and less likely to become overweight than rats limited to a cage environment. You can be certain that your rat would love feeling the grass on his belly and sniffing around rocks as well as running around on the carpet. Imagine the looks you'll get from your neighbors and passersby as they see you walking your rat. Well, you chose to be a rat owner—what did you expect?

Before you take your rat outdoors, undertake the necessary training to ensure his safety. Unconstrained and untrained, Ben and Ira are unlikely to remain near you when there is a whole

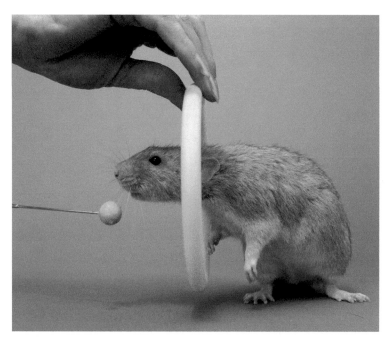

Equipment you will need for leash training include a target stick and a hoop, which are used to teach your rat to accept a harness.

world to explore and tempting objects to test for edibility. And don't expect to be able to catch a rat scooting off on an adventure. You need to be confident that your rat will come to you when he must, and you need enough control to make sure your rat isn't endangered by vehicles, fast-moving feet, or animals that are more likely to perceive him as a meal than a playmate. To that end, we need to teach Ben and Ira to first accept a harness and then willingly walk with you on a leash.

Acclimating Ben and Ira to a harness may be difficult, as rats don't like being confined against their will. However, they do like small, tight spaces and will acclimate, provided they are introduced to the harness properly without being frightened. That means breaking down the process into small, nonthreatening steps.

Draw the stick back as your rat approaches so that he goes all the way through the hoop.

Harness Training

We'll begin by teaching your rat to go through a hoop. Then we'll gradually decrease the diameter of the hoop until it's barely wider than the diameter of the rat's abdomen. The next step is setting up two to three of these hoops and teaching your rat to move through them on command. Once your rat is consistently successful and comfortable performing this behavior, we'll introduce the harness to the routine, teaching the rat to move through a hoop and then through the harness. Finally, we'll work on training your rat to go into his harness on command and remain still while you make the harness snug.

Move Through a Hoop

Begin with a hoop made of metal or plastic. The hoop's diameter should be wide enough that your rat can easily pass through without touching the sides or top. First, allow Ben and Ira to get used to the feel and scent of the hoop. Put a few food morsels down so that the rats will want to approach and investigate. Click the moment they are moving over the side of the hoop and reward.

1. Hold the hoop vertically, with its bottom point resting on the floor or tabletop.

2. Your rat should be on one side; tap your finger or target stick on the surface on the other side, very close to where the rat will have to pass through the hoop.

3. By now Ben and Ira should be well conditioned to come to a tap, so they should show immediate response and come toward it.

4. The tricky part is making sure the rats come to the target through the hoop and not around it. If you are having problems with this, place the hoop between two solid boards about 8 inches wide. This will ensure success.

5. Repeat this exercise until Ben and Ira go directly through the hoop to your tapping finger, without hesitating or going around.

Hoops can be made of the nylon leash to acclimate your rat to a future body harness.

The next step is to gradually decrease the diameter of the hoop, thus leading your rat to pass through a smaller and smaller space to reach his destination. Practice with successively smaller hoops until Ben and Ira are very comfortable moving through something that touches the sides of their bodies. This is important because a harness will caress their sides, too. This step shouldn't be difficult, since rats prefer to move against something solid, at least on one side.

Once your rat is comfortable with the hoop, take a couple of lengths of nylon rope and coil it into loops. You can also use your leash, which is normally made of the same material as the

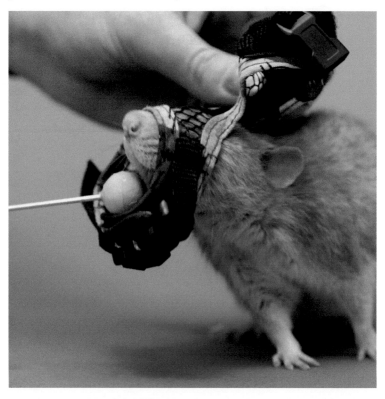

You can lure your rat through the harness in the same way you did through the hoop; once he's used to a small hoop, the transfer to a harness should be easy.

harness. Begin by presenting one loop held open with your fingertips for your rat to move through it. Gradually decrease the diameter of the loop until Ben and Ira brush their sides against the material as they go through.

When your rats are completely comfortable moving through the material loop, present them with multiple material coils so that they must move through two or three loops to reach their reward.

Whenever you present a new part of this behavior, be certain to back off on your criteria a little. For example, decrease the amount of distance between the rat and his reward so that the rat reaches it quickly once he is successful in the new hoop arrangement. As Ben becomes comfortable moving through it, increase the distance between the rat and the hoop as well as between the hoop and the food morsel. Eventually Ben and Ira will be running to you to put on their harnesses!

Move into the Harness

Once your rats consistently move through a series of material hoops, begin familiarizing them with the harness. Allow Ben and Ira to sniff the harness, but make sure that the rats don't chew on it. You don't want your rats to think the harness is a chew toy. Ben and Ira must learn to ignore it, for the most part, and not try to remove or eat it. If your rats have a real problem with this, spraying something icky on the material—bitter apple or jalapeño juice should deter the behavior.

Practice having Ben and Ira move through the harness as they did with the plastic and material hoops. Do this several times or until your rat is very comfortable moving directly through the contraption to obtain the reward.

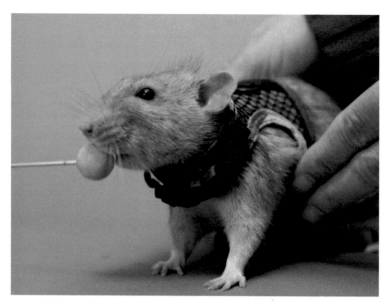

Continue targeting as you or a friend secures the harness.

Now we need to get Ben and Ira accustomed to having the harness tightened snugly around their bodies. You'll be more successful if you place a food dish containing little treats at one end of the harness and tap that as a cue for your rats to come through.

Position the dish just at the front edge of the harness so that as soon as Ben's head peeks through, he can dip it down into the dish of food. As he's gorging himself, gradually tighten the harness until it is snug. If your rat has any reaction to this, back off a little, but take the food away when you loosen the harness. Ben must earn that dish of treats. Try again later. Leave your rat wanting more instead of running away from you.

Practice the harnessing exercise every day at least once. When your rat is comfortable wearing his harness, practice other previously learned behaviors, this time in harness. This will help him understand that he can still move about freely and do all the fun tricks he wants,

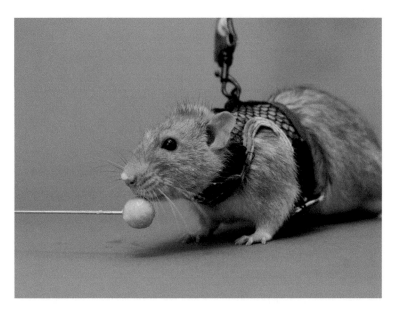

Now we're ready to go for a walk! Lure your rat forward using the target stick.

and the entire process will remain positive. Before long, wearing the harness will become just another part of your rat's routine.

Walk with a Waddle

It's time to waddle in step. In other words, your rat waddles alongside as you walk with him, a leash attached to his harness. Make sure you take little steps, as Ben's and Ira's legs are very short. Rats can move surprisingly fast, but when confronted with an unfamiliar environment, they will take it slow, sniffing things as they go along. Rats rarely rush headlong into new situations or stuff themselves on new foods. They investigate and learn along the way.

Since your rat is very small and you are relatively very tall, teaching your pet to walk with a waddle is best achieved by utilizing a very long target stick, approximately 3 feet in length. This tool

The target stick will keep your rat moving with you; begin the leash-walking exercise indoors.

allows you to keep the target at rat level without requiring you to bend over or stoop for extended periods. I often use this technique when training small dogs or cats as well as rats and recommend it for anyone who, like me, wants to avoid back strain from bending to slowly move the target that is teaching the animal to remain at my side. It is also good reinforcement to walk the same way in training—upright—that you'll eventually walk outdoors.

We'll begin our walk training by putting on the harness. Allow your rat to wear the harness for about fifteen minutes prior to the walk. Always keep an eye on your pet. If he is prone to nibbling on the harness, keep him busy. Don't worry about getting your own things together, such as house keys, hat, sweater, or wallet, as we're remaining indoors for a while. We need to make certain that your rat understands how to walk on a leash before he is exposed to the myriad distractions of the great outdoors. Once you take a rat outside, he will never be the same. He will want to go out every chance he gets. Indoor cats have similar reactions. It's a very inviting new world to the keen senses of these animals. At this point, however, even an indoor walk will capture your pet's interest; as your rat has been relegated to specific areas of your house, a walk through the entire area will be a new and enjoyable experience.

Before you begin, outfit yourself as a mobile rat-training facility. Hold the target stick and clicker in the hand on the side of your body at which your rat will be walking. Hold the leash in the opposite hand, or tie it around a belt loop. Wear a pouch filled with rat goodies. Bring a variety of yummies with variable ratings—a piece of lab block for a fairly good rat behavior, a Cheerio for a slightly better rat reaction, and yogurt raisins for a rat that is so wrapped up in whatever you do that he ignores a really inviting distraction.

Don't expect to make the entire round of your home within the first walk. You need to take one step at a time to be sure that your rat is walking with you and not being dragged by you. Your rat must learn to associate being on the leash with great adventures, not a tug-of-war.

1. Stand upright, holding the leash and target stick as described above. Put the stick near enough to your rat that he will reach out to touch the target with his nose. Click and drop a treat for him, as close as possible to the point where he touched the target stick.

2. Take a step forward, luring your rat with the target stick. As he catches up to the stick and touches it with his nose, click and reward.

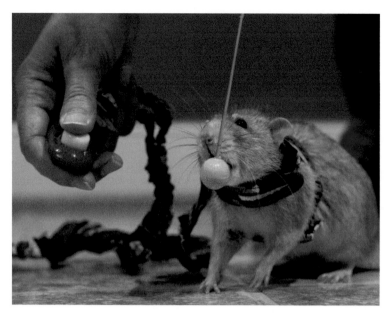

Hold the target stick in your left hand and leash with clicker in your right hand. Take small steps, and reward each increment.

3. Take another step forward. Repeat step 2 up to three times.
4. Take two steps. Wait for your pet to catch up and touch the target stick. Click and reward.
5. Repeat step 4 up to three times.
6. Repeating the sequence as above, taking three steps between each touch-click-reward sequence.

As your rat learns to walk with you, take more and more steps between the pause when you click and reward. However, I recommend taking no more than five to six steps at any given time, as it takes a while for your rat to catch up with you (unless you walk at a snail's pace, in which case your pet might forge ahead a little).

So, you've walked the house, and it's time to return Ben to his cage. You need to teach him how to turn around. This is done by luring with the target stick. Just as you were able to lure your rat forward, you can also lure him through a turn.

1. Present Ben with the target stick. He'll reach out to touch it. Just before he can do so, move it partially around a turn. Not all the way. That's too much at one time. Just a third to half of the way around.
2. When Ben arrives and touches the target, click and reward.
3. Complete the turn, luring with the target stick. Click and reward as soon as Ben touches the stick. Then walk forward a few steps, stop, click, and reward when he catches up.

Use the target stick to teach your rat to turn.

Now that you and your rat can walk the length of your entire house, it's time to go outside. Be sure that the harness is very secure and that your pet rat is walking with you willingly, without trying to get out of his harness.

1. Carry Ben outdoors. Find a comfortable spot in the shade and sit down. Allow your rat to climb off of you and explore the immediate area while you sit calmly. Don't let go of the leash.
2. Every time Ben returns to you, click and reward. If, by chance, he touches the target stick, click and reward.
3. The first four to five times you go outdoors, repeat the previous steps, increasing the duration each time but not attempting to walk. Ben will be so thrilled to be in such a rich environment that he'll be very busy— indeed, far too busy to concentrate on walking with you.
4. Once your rat is comfortable being outdoors, try to have him walk with you just a few steps. See how this goes. Is Ben following along, nose aiming for the target stick, or is he taking his sweet time and waddling along, sniffing the grass, bugs, trash, and animal markers?

If your rat is paying attention to the target, you can take a few more steps. If not, be happy that he is meandering along at his own speed and having a great time. Your pet will catch up to you eventually. Then again, if he senses something really interesting, you may be trying to catch up with him.

As with any behavior, the more you practice, the better and more durable the response. If you plan on taking Ben and Ira for long walks through the neighborhood, be prepared for many

Allow some time for your rat to acclimate to the floor; a long stick will be helpful to you.

weeks of work before you can go all the way around the block in less than two hours. It's unrealistic to expect to ever walk your rat as you would walk your dog. Rats' very short legs mean they move very close to the ground, much like a Basset Hound whose nose is made to skim the ground. Similarly, a rat's keen sense of smell makes it difficult for him to pass up an interesting scent, and he shouldn't be hurried.

7

Scurry and Hurry

This rat is learning to sit up—one of the training behaviors you will want to teach him.

Now that Ben and Ira come when called and can walk with you and your target stick, you can progress to training some really fun behaviors! As a professional rat trainer for film and television, I have taught these clever critters to perform stunts of great skill and daring. I am happy to share my methods with you, but if you don't feel fully confident you can re-create these behaviors safely, don't despair. There are enough low-risk tricks in these pages to keep you and Ira busy for ages. In this chapter, you'll learn how to train your rat to stand on his hind legs, negotiate obstacles of all sorts, stay in one location, and ride on your shoulder—plus how to link several behaviors so that your rat will perform many different commands for a single treat.

This is called behavior chaining—combining two or more behaviors prior to marking the moment of completion. You've actually already done this with teaching your rat to turn his head, move toward your tap, and wait for his reward. That was a chain of behavioral events. Now, with just a bit more time and effort, your rat might *really* impress!

Atten-Hut!

Training your rat to stand on his hind legs is probably easier than teaching him to come when called. Standing upright, balanced on his hind legs, is one of the rat's natural postures. It helps the rat to reach things and see over obstacles. If you feed your rat with tongs, you can hold the food over his head. Automatically, the rat will reach up for the food. As he does so, click and give him the food. This trick is easiest with lab blocks, fruit, and vegetables, which are big enough for you to easily hold with tongs and for your rat to grab.

As your rats are familiar with the concept of target luring, teaching Ben and Ira to stand on their hind legs should be a cinch. Gradually shape the behavior as follows:

1. Tap the end of the target stick, signaling your rat to come to the target.
2. Once he arrives, click and reward.
3. Move the target a short distance, and tap again.
4. Upon the rat's arrival, click and reward.
5. Tap the target stick on the surface until you gain your rat's attention. Then hold the end a few inches off the surface so that the rat must lift his head up to touch the stick.
6. Click and reward the moment he touches the target stick.

Gradually increase the distance between the stick and the working surface. For example, begin with 2 inches, then repeat the exercise from 3 inches. When your rat performs consistently with the target stick 3 inches from the working surface, move to 4 inches. Never try to push your rat beyond his limits by holding the stick way out of reach. This will extinguish your rat's desire to perform. Don't expect your rat to reach beyond reason. Until he is good at the behavior, in fact, your limit should be no higher than your rat's body length (not including his tail).

Rat Agility

Ever watch dogs run through an agility course? They walk over high boards, A-frames, and seesaws; weave through poles; jump over obstacles; and go through tunnels. When a rat goes through a maze and figures out which direction to take to obtain a reward, he is performing an exercise very similar to that performed by a canine on an agility course. There's no reason why you can't add some rat-size obstacles to the routine to have some fun with your rodent.

Because rats are very agile and love to investigate new places, you can make the obstacles as large as you wish. However, if you are expecting your rat to jump over mountains, forget it. Rats are very good at leaping but don't generally leap very high, and they'll rarely leap over an obstacle they can climb over. If you are planning on making some rat jumps, you'll want something close to the ground and sturdy—this isn't stadium jumping, after all.

You can, however, make obstacles that require climbing as tall as you like. Rats can easily climb almost any surface. They are especially agile rope climbers, an ability no dog can match. There's no need to spend a lot of money, for you can make an entire obstacle course with rope alone.

Lure Ben to the opening of the tunnel.

Place the tip of the target stick in the far end of the tube to draw him in.

Lure Ben all the way through, then click and reward. Following food into the tunnel makes it even more fun for the rat. Treasure hunt!

A tunnel can be made of pipe cleaners and cloth, or you can buy some large-diameter PVC pipe. The great advantage of PVC is that it comes premade in a wide range of widths and corner fittings, so you can make an entire maze out of one material. PVC tubing is also very easy to clean: just rinse and dry. Another great feature is that your rat will not likely chew on it as he would on cloth. Cloth makes great nesting material. Plastic is not as comfortable.

I also suggest making weave poles out of PVC, as any wood product will likely be chewed. The half-inch-diameter pipe works well for this purpose. For outdoor play, poke it into soft ground. For an indoor course, glue it to a thick board.

Should you want to have your rat exercise outdoors, excellent barriers are now on the market that keep small animals within a 20-cubic-foot area. The material is a strip of sleek plastic that can be attached with Velcro at the ends, giving you and your little ones a great area to play in safety. Think of all the fun you can have setting up the little agility course and running your rat through!

This rat is exploring a colorful store-bought plastic tunnel.

Ben and Ira can be easily taught to negotiate any agility obstacle through luring, one step at a time. The speed at which your rat learns how to go over, through, or under something depends on his food drive, as you will be luring him a few steps, clicking and rewarding when he arrives, then luring him a few more steps. I'd suggest you conduct a training session prior to offering a meal or use the feeding time itself as a training session. Rats would much rather actively search for their meals than have food handed to them. After all, isn't it more fun to search for treasure than to have it plopped in front of you?

To train Ben to go through tunnels, place a very short tunnel, one even shorter than your target stick, on the working surface. Position yourself at the exit end and slide the target stick through the tunnel so that the end extends through the entrance. Tap the end of the target stick to get Ben's attention. As he comes toward the tunnel, retract the stick to the entrance. Click and reward as Ben goes to the entrance. Next, pull the stick through the tunnel a little ways, close enough so to you that you can reach in with a piece of food once Ben is halfway through. As you draw the target stick all the way through the exit, with rat in tow, click and reward again. After repeating this procedure a couple of times, you should be able to merely tap the tunnel, and your rat will go through it to get his food on the other side.

Repeat the tunnel acclimation exercise using several different tunnel configurations—say, a couple of straightaways of different lengths connected by some corners. Gradually add more pieces. When Ben is readily going through one assembly, add another part. Within a fairly short time, you should have a great tunneling rat.

If Ben and Ira ever show reluctance to go into a tunnel, merely place a morsel of food inside. You could leave a trail of little bits all through the tunnel, giving your rat positive associations with going into the small, tight space—not that Ben and Ira will need much prodding, as rats normally love going into small, darkened spaces. Once the rats are comfortable in the section containing food morsels, you will easily be able to transfer the positive associations to other parts of the tunnel system.

Now let's put together an entire agility course. We need to combine all the different obstacles that your rat has learned to negotiate one at a time. You can begin by chaining two obstacles. When Ben and Ira reliably and successfully traverse these two, add another. Continue in this manner until you have designed an entire agility course, and your rats are having a great time negotiating all the obstacles for one click and reward. Your rats will be having so much fun that the activity becomes its own reward.

Riding High

What's more fun than walking around with a rat on your shoulder? Not only does a shoulder-riding rat give you ease of mobility,

Two rats are twice the fun of one—especially when it comes to shoulder rides.

but the novelty of your little pet is also sure to draw glances from passersby. If you've been walking your rat on a leash through the neighborhood, you should be used to the attention by now.

Rats love to explore their world. Going on a shoulder-riding journey is a real thrill. But before you plop your rat on your shoulder and take off, you must prepare Ben and Ira for the experience and take some safety precautions.

First, Ben needs to learn how to remain in one spot for extended periods of time. It simply won't do to have your rat crawling all over you as you move about. He might fall!

You'll need to teach your rat to respond to the *stay* command. This is done through a very gradual shaping process, using your target stick or a small piece of cloth.

As most rats, especially females, naturally prefer moving around to sitting still, it might take a while to teach the *stay* command. Be patient, and reward the minor increments. In time, with consistent training, you'll succeed.

Begin by deciding whether you want to teach your rat to remain on a piece of cloth or to target on the stick. You'll need to carry whichever target you choose with you when you move around so that Ben and Ira will have consistent cues to respond to.

Teach your rat to go to a specific material in order to begin teaching the *stay* or *go to* commands (washcloths work great).

Ira will learn to go to his mark faster if you teach him through targeting.

The training procedure depends on the target you use. Let's assume you use the target stick.

1. Place the stick on the working surface, tapping the end to attract Ben's attention. When the rat arrives, click and reward.
2. Move the target stick a little. Don't tap it. Wait.
3. When your rat touches the stick, immediately click and reward.
4. Move it again a short distance.
5. This time, when your rat moves to touch the end of the stick, don't click right away. Wait a couple of seconds, then click and reward.
6. Gradually increase the time your rat remains in place before you click and reward. Remember that you can't take huge jumps in time. Increase the delay in 1-second increments.

Placing food on the cloth marker will make your rat believe that the marker is a very positive place to be.

If you reach a point—say, after 5 seconds—when Ben begins to move away from the target stick, back up to clicking after he holds the position for 4 seconds. Do three to five repetitions. When he's comfortable remaining in place for 4 seconds, try the 5-second increment again. Sometimes, you have to regress in your criteria before you can progress in your training.

Now, let's try this exercise using a piece of brightly colored cloth as a target. This target might be the better choice if you intend to move around while your rat is on your shoulder. Holding a target stick against your shoulder is far more difficult than pinning the cloth to your shirt. A cloth target also gives your rat something besides your shirt to cling to as you move.

1. Place the piece of cloth on the working surface.
2. Put a morsel of food on the cloth.
3. When Ira puts a foot on the cloth, click and allow him to have the food morsel.

This rat has learned that the cloth marker brings great things.

4. Repeat step 3 four or five times.
5. Move the piece of cloth and wait.
6. When Ira places his front feet on the cloth, click and reward. Repeat this step four or five times, then move the cloth again.

Once Ira is readily going to the cloth and waiting for his food, it's time to teach him to wait for the click. Gradually increase the amount of time he must remain on the cloth before you click and reward. Increase the delay in 1-second increments, just as you would using a target stick.

Once your rat readily goes to its target zone and remains there for short periods of time (e.g., 15 seconds), place the target on a different surface and work on the same exercise. Choose a place that is not quite level and is fairly narrow, such as the back of a chair or couch—the point is to prepare your rat for riding on your similarly sloped shoulder.

The cloth marker can be placed anywhere, and the rat learns to remain on the cloth.

Now we're ready for the big event. Place your rat on your shoulder. Once he's in the right location, either on the piece of cloth or near your target stick, click and give him a food morsel. Repeat this four or five times. Gradually increase the amount of time between clicks and treats.

When your rat comfortably and reliably remains in one place on your shoulder for at least 20 seconds, begin walking around. Move very slowly at first and try not to lean or in any way give your rat a rocky ride. No one likes to drive with someone who can't shift the transmission smoothly. After walking a few seconds, stop, click, and reward your rat. Gradually increase the amount of movement as you increase the length of time your pet remains perched on your shoulder.

You're almost ready to take the circus outdoors. Before you do, take appropriate safety precautions. You never know when your rat might fall or purposely skitter off to investigate some-thing irresistible, so put Ira's harness on before you go outdoors.

Tie the leash to a belt loop or around your wrist. Bring your clicker, food morsels, and a pouch to carry it all. You'll want something that offers easy access to the food without having to search. Looking for the food takes your mind off what your rat is up to. When outside, it's very important that you are always aware of Ira's antics.

As in all new situations, gradually increase the length of time you spend walking outdoors with your rat. Gradually introduce your rat to situations with more distractions as well. Starting your walks in a busy neighborhood or on a busy street is a great way to frighten your rat. Begin on a quiet side street or cul-de-sac. When Ben is comfortable there, go somewhere with more people and other distractions. Overstimulating your rat on his first outing will only make him want to hide in your pocket instead of looking at the world perched on your shoulder.

The cloth can even be placed on your shoulder if you want to teach your rat to remain in one place instead of burrowing through your hair. Pin it to your shirt for a secure perch.

This is the best view in the house.

Extreme Ride

Once Ben and Ira are seasoned shoulder riders, you can begin teaching them more extreme shoulder-riding sports. How about taking them with you to outdoor fairs and sports activities? Or allowing them to ride shotgun as you do yardwork? Some rat owners have even trained their pets to stay on their shoulder while they skateboard or ride a bike, although these activities certainly pose more of a risk to your rider.

Rats get bored as easily as humans do. Who can be satisfied with a mere walk around the block? Add new adventures to the basic shoulder ride, and your rats will get more out of the experience.

The key is gradual acclimation. If your goal is to ride a skateboard with Ben on your shoulder, begin with short, straight, level courses on wheels. Hang on tightly to his leash, keeping it short enough so that if he does fall, he won't hit the ground and risk being run over. As he learns to relax and enjoy the movement, add variations such as going backward, turning, and eventually going off ramps. Never do flips and leaps, however, which require total concentration on your own body position and render you incapable of safeguarding your rat.

CHAPTER

8

Dogs, Cats, and Rats, Oh My!

Teach your dog to pay attention to you before you introduce him to your rat. Always reinforce good behavior.

ALL PETS CAN LEARN TO GET ALONG AND LIVE TOGETHER within a peaceable household kingdom, but harmony depends totally on you, your training of each animal, your diligent observation, and your understanding of each animal's unique acclimation time. If you choose to own a menagerie, take the time to first prepare each member and then maintain the simple rules of management.

Let's begin with preparing your other pets, the dog and the cat, to live harmoniously with your rat. Only when you're certain that those larger animals won't make lunch out of Ben should you introduce him to them (and some of you may never feel certain). Your naturally curious and cautious rodent will quickly accept your other animals provided he doesn't receive any

This cat hardly notices his more curious rat companion.

threatening vibes. But no matter what your level of comfort is, *never* allow your animals to interact without close supervision.

Dog Friends

Most dogs will easily learn to accept rats as housemates as long as they don't have any bad experiences. However, you will need to teach your dog to behave with this added distraction. The focus of this book permits only a brief description of the training your dog should get—at the very least, you should teach Fido to remain in a sit or down-stay even in the event that a scurrying creature shoots up his leg and perches on top of his head. Until you can count on that obedient response, Fido could react by sending Brer Rat flying with a forceful toss of his head. Not a great way to start a relationship!

You will begin by luring your dog into position; then, click and reward when he does what you wish and work on shaping the behavior into a faster and stronger response.

The Sit

Show your dog a treat. When he goes for it, click or say "Good dog!" and give him the treat. Repeat this four or five times.

Hold the treat between Fido's eyes, and lure him into looking upward. As he looks up, his rear end will go down. Praise, or click and give him a treat. Repeat this four or five times, then add the cue "Fido, sit." When he does so, praise and reward.

Gradually increase the amount of time he must remain sitting prior to praising or clicking. This will help teach Fido patience as well as how to stay in the sitting position. The increments should be 3–5 seconds. Dogs don't require the same split-second timing that a rat requires.

When Fido can remain in a sit for at least 10 seconds, add the cue "Fido, stay." Gradually increase each stay time. If he should get up before you've rewarded him, lure him back into position, and greatly shorten the amount of time you make him stay. Then gradually lengthen it again.

Your dog should be reliable for at least 1 minute of sit and stay before you introduce him to Ben and Ira. It's also a good idea to put Fido on a leash during these initial greetings. You need some way to control Fido when you present him with something he might consider a moving meal.

The Down

Once you have taught Fido to sit and stay, he's ready to learn how to lie down and stay. This is a very important behavior, since dogs can maintain a longer stay in the down position, and it's harder for dogs to scramble to their feet when they are lying down than when they are sitting.

1. Show Fido the treat under his nose as he sits.
2. Lower the treat directly below his nose. When he lowers his head to get the treat, click and/or praise and give him the treat.
3. Ask him to lower his head a little more the next time. Gradually, ask him to lower his body more and more with each request. Within a short time, Fido should be fully lying down.
4. Now it's time to give the cue command for the down. Say, "Fido, down," as you show him the treat and lure him into position. Praise and/or click, and give him his treat.
5. When Fido is comfortable lying down on command, add the stay exercise following the same procedure you used in teaching the sit.

Again, prior to introducing Ben and Ira, make certain Fido is comfortable with maintaining a down-stay for a couple of minutes. Use a leash in case of an emergency, such as "I can't possibly stay here a moment longer with that little rascal cavorting all over my body."

It will take some time for Fido to fully accept Ben and Ira. Don't rush things. Begin with small increments, and build on the success of these instead of leaving anything to chance.

Cat and Rat

This is potentially the more difficult situation because cats are notorious, natural rodent exterminators. Telling a cat to hold still when a meal on wheels is nearby simply might be too much to demand of any self-respecting cat. Few cats can learn to ignore such fair game—that would be tantamount to asking a teenager to ignore a hand-held gaming system loaded with the latest shoot-'em-up.

The best tack to take with cats and rats is separation. Don't leave them together—especially not loose—when you aren't present. If Fluffy manages to get into the rat room, at least Ben and Ira will be safe in their cages. A proper rat cage won't allow Fluffy to penetrate it with more than a claw, and as your rats may be curious about that claw, Fluffy might learn that intruding claws receive protruding teeth, a valuable lesson.

If you insist on trying to make friends out of Fluffy and Ben, you will need to place some form of restraint on your cat. A body harness would be best. However, keep in mind that a harness won't stop Fluffy from reaching out with those quick, clawed paws. In the case of rats and cats, precaution is best.

Be extra alert when introducing your rat to your cat. Note that kittens are generally more accepting of rats than are older felines.

Tweety and Petey

As with any interaction among animals, there is always a risk of conflict resulting in possible injury. Many reliable sources do not recommend interactions between birds and rats, but in my years of training, I have had few if any problems. They generally steer clear of each other. Then again, Petey the rat might be great stimulation for Tweety the bird. After all, they like to play with the same kinds of toys. Additionally, unless Tweety is a hawk, owl, or other meat-eating bird, neither animal will wish to make lunch of the other. As both pets require a lot of stimulation, they can offer each other great companionship. Should Tweety be a talking bird, he will most likely learn rat lingo in no time.

Both Tweety and Petey can learn to perform all sorts of new behaviors in much the same way—using positive reinforcement and shaping techniques. For each behavior you wish to teach, break the ultimate goal into smaller, discrete, achievable steps. As your pet accomplishes each minor goal, begin to string them together using behavior chaining. This means that you require your pet to perform more than one behavior in order to earn the click and reward. With consistency and patience, you will reach your goals with both pets.

Getting to Know You

As you have learned, rats fit into almost any household. Even if you have cats, there are ways to ensure the safety of the animals while enjoying their company. You must take the time to acclimate the animals to each other with caution and constant observation. Make certain that those animals that might harm Ben and Ira are harnessed and controlled before you expose them to your rats. The meeting should be a positive experience. Follow the steps I've outlined below to help teach the animals that the presence of the other brings great rewards—from you.

1. Before bringing out your rat, make sure that your other pet is not only well trained but also securely harnessed.
2. If your other pet is a dog, place Fido in a down-stay.
3. Have another family member bring out Ben.
4. As Fido notices Ben, keep Fido in his stay position using click-and-reward techniques. Repeat your click and reward every couple of seconds as Fido redirects his attention from Ben to you. After all, you, not the rat, are the treat dispenser.

You can also use the same procedures with a cat or bird. However, understand that cats (and terrier-breed dogs) have very powerful prey drives against rodents. Begin the introduction from a distance at which the presence of the rat doesn't trigger a strong reaction. As your larger pet learns to not react to Ira's presence, bring him a step closer. With each increment, continually praise and reward your larger pet. Your rat will probably not react to the other animal until he is very close. If Ben hasn't had a bad experience with Fido, he will not react fearfully when introduced—unless he sees big teeth chomping in his direction.

The moment you see your larger pet show a bit of interest in Ben, observe the reaction carefully. Does Fido look back to you for reinforcement? Or is Ben a more reinforcing reward? Make certain that you are offering Fido a higher-value choice. If a bit of kibble isn't more interesting than rat meat, try using cheese or freeze-dried liver. If your pet shows too much interest in Ben, have the person holding the rat back up a few steps to the point at which your larger pet showed more interest in you than in a rat chase. Work at this distance for a while until Fido or Fluffy would rather pay attention to you.

You will need to spend several training sessions of about a half hour each to gradually acclimate Fido to Ben and Fluffy to Ira. If you are working with Tweety and Petey, it may not require as much acclimation time, especially if you keep their cages in visual proximity to each other.

Even when you have successfully brought larger pets close enough to your rat to fully see and smell each other, you still need to continually monitor the larger animal's behavior while in the presence of the rodent. When you see your dog or cat turn his attention away from your rat and back to you, click and reward every time. You are in the process of conditioning Fido and Fluffy to come to you for rewards instead of seeking the self-rewarding behavior of making a meal of Ben. Instinctive behavior is very difficult to redirect, so you must be diligent and consistent. Even the slightest turn of the head in your direction should be rewarded.

Now we get to some fun things to do with Fido and Ben. Don't try these things with Fluffy and the rat. Cats are very fast, and unless you are a professional trainer with quick reflexes, it is far too risky to work the animals together.

Fun with Fido and Ben

Now that Fido and Ben are friends, you can work with them together and teach them some fun tricks. Fido can learn to lie still with Ben walking on him, and Ben can learn to ride around on Fido (provided Fido is not racing around the yard). In fact, Ben can learn to ride around on anything; a dog is just another means of transportation, the rodent version of an extreme sport.

Place the cloth in a secure area of the remote-controlled vehicle.

Allow your rat to investigate the new toy.

Let's begin with teaching Ben to "drive." Now, one must have a license to ride the big wheels. We'll begin with earning the learner's permit with a small wagon. Once your rat has earned his permit, we'll give him the experience he needs to ride in the driver's seat. When he's very good at remaining in his seat as the vehicle is moving, he'll be ready to learn to ride the elephant (Fido).

Learner's Permit

You'll need a small wagon for this training exercise. A manually operated wheeled vehicle is best in the beginning. You can control the movement and speed while keeping an eye on Ben. Line the bed of the wagon with a nonslip material that your rat can grip to prevent him from sliding around. Ben will not like riding around with you if he's sliding all over his seat. In fact, he might become very frightened. Try using a bathtub mat or rubber-backed carpet. This will give your rat traction while offering him a soft seat.

Now for the easiest part of the game. Simply place your rat in the wagon and give him a little food. Pull him forward a few feet. Click and give him another morsel of food. Gradually increase the distance you pull between each click and reward. Now Ben has learned that riding around in a wagon is pretty fun and earns him lots of rewards.

The next step is to teach Ben to remain at a specific spot while riding around. This is called staying on a mark. The mark can be a piece of cloth or a piece of tape that is a different color from the overall surface. Whatever the material, make certain it stands out from the surrounding area in both color and texture.

We need to shape your rat into remaining in this one spot, or staying on the mark, on your cue. This must be done very gradually and will be far more time consuming than just riding around. But the training is worthwhile because of what you will have to look forward to: once Ben understand *stay on the mark*, you can have him do this anywhere. Remember how we went over this in order to have your rat ride safely on your shoulder? It's the same concept, only the rat is not on you but on a vehicle that you control.

1. Lure Ben to the spot by placing a morsel of food on it and tapping.
2. When he goes to the food, click and allow him to eat the morsel.
3. Repeat this sequence at least three times.

Ben will soon learn to go to the mark for his reward. He might even go there without your giving the specific cue of tapping the spot. When he does so, it is time to teach him to remain in that spot for a short period. On his arrival, make him wait a couple seconds, then click and give him his treat. Gradually increase the amount of time he is to wait for his click and reward.

Move the mark to the seat of a remote-controlled vehicle. I'd suggest a truck so that there's plenty of space for Ben to sit safely. Teach your rat to go to the driver's seat when you tap the surface. As he is already familiar with the tap, meaning to come, and the mark as the destination he is to reach, the transition should be fairly easy.

Driving Practice

Now that your rat knows how to sit still in the driver's seat, it's time to get moving. At first, stay very close to the remote-controlled vehicle in case your rat decides that he doesn't much

Begin any movement manually until your rat acclimates to the motion. Remain close and offer lots of reinforcement during the initial test drives.

We're now ready for the truck rally.

care for motoring down the hallway. If he shows signs of stress or tries to dismount, you must be there to either lure him back onto his mark or redirect him into another behavior. Otherwise, the rat will develop a very negative attitude toward driving and run in the opposite direction when he sees those wheels.

When Ben is staying comfortably in his spot, manually move the little car forward about 6 inches. If he remains on board, click and give him a reward. Repeat this step until Ben is riding along as though he were born to drive. Then manually move the vehicle about a foot at a time. Try to maintain a smooth motion as your rat is sure to dislike jerky stops and starts. He won't look forward to training sessions filled with whiplash.

Now that Ben is comfortable riding around a couple feet at a time, you can begin using the remote control from a great distance. Be certain to follow along, however, so that you can click and reward often. If Ben doesn't feel that the ride is worth the rewards, he'll promptly exit the vehicle. I also suggest that you maintain a very slow speed. Your rat isn't wearing a helmet and safety goggles, nor is he strapped in with a seat belt. Be safe. Be courteous, and watch where you steer. All it takes is one mishap, and you may never get your rat to drive again.

Elephant Seat (or, Riding the Dog)

Ben can easily make the transition from riding on a remote-controlled vehicle to riding on Fido (as long as all possible safety precautions are employed). The main focus of your training in this exercise will be Fido. Will he accept walking around with Ben on his head or shoulders? You might want to try this with a small stuffed toy first. This will give your dog a chance to

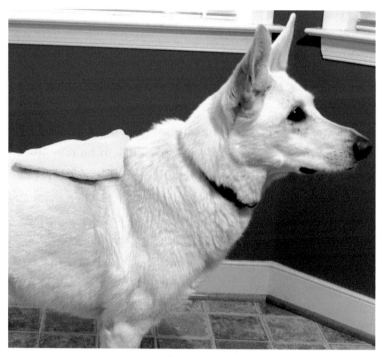

You can initially use a toy or cloth marker to get Fido used to having something on his back. The cloth will also teach your rat to remain in place.

acclimate to carrying something while he moves around. Once he accepts this, the rat will not be much of an issue, especially if Fido gets lots of clicks and treats.

Begin by putting Ben's movable mark on your dog. You might need to anchor it at Fido's collar so that the mark is attached and available for Ben to cling to while Fido is ambling about. Rats have a very good grip, so this shouldn't be an issue, especially if the mark is made of cloth. Instead of allowing Ben to crawl to his mark on Fido, you should place him in position, then click and reward as he settles in.

Begin with the simple click and reward as Ben remains on Fido, on his mark. Gradually increase the amount of time

Once everyone is ready, it's time to go for a (slow) ride.

between the clicks, teaching Ben to remain in place for longer and longer periods. When he is staying for more than two minutes, it's time to begin walking Fido around a bit.

Keep your dog on a leash during these beginning stages. Closely monitor the situation, and be ready to take hold of Ben before he falls or tries to leave his seat while Fido's still in motion. Again, your rat's not wearing a seat belt, so you must be there to help. You'll also want to keep Fido at a slow pace at first. Both Fido and Ben are still acclimating to the situation and each other.

As Fido and Ben get to know each other and enjoy each other's company, there's no end to the adventures. I'm certain that with a little imagination you can come up with some new ideas for all of your pets.

CHAPTER

9

The Great Rat Race

Once your rat is trained, you can take him out of his cage and into the wider world. A talented rat can be a great travel companion and a fierce sports competitor—and even an actor.

Now that Ben and Ira know all these great tricks, what next? Time to show off!

Think about the things you enjoy. A bike ride? Traveling to visit family and friends? Hiking in the woods? Going to the movies? How about the Xtreme Rat Challenge? Rats can be a welcome addition to any activity. In fact, they are very good travelers.

Have Rat, Will Travel

Traveling with your rat is very easy. You rarely have to make special arrangements as you would for a larger pet. Ben and Ira can be transported in a small, hard carrier supplied at all times with food and water. They're small enough to store under an airline seat or in a large carrying bag. They won't make much noise, either. That means other passengers will hardly know you're traveling with rodents. Just be certain that your rats don't get jostled about, or they might become very stressed. A stressed rat is more susceptible to airborne contagions, as their immune systems weaken. Don't allow them to go nose to nose with any other animals. You don't know what diseases unknown creatures might be carrying.

You should also be very cautious when deciding whether to allow other people to hold your rat. Humans carry germs on their hands. If you want to allow others to enjoy the company of Ben and Ira while you travel, bring along some antibacterial hand sanitizer. Once the person's hands are clean, he or she can hold your precious rodent as long as you (and Ben) will allow. However, permit this handling only in an enclosed area, as one big rat leap can mean hours of chasing down your friend in a busy airport or train terminal. That can be a nightmare!

Because traveling is unavoidably stressful, I recommend that time spent outside of the rats' cage en route be kept to a minimum. Airlines have rules about allowing pets out of their carriers. In fact, they often don't allow it at all. If you are traveling by bus, train, or automobile, it is safest for Ben and Ira to remain in their carrier, as you never know when the vehicle will have to stop suddenly or might go over a pothole, sending your rats flying out of your hands and onto the lap of a very surprised person in front of you. That can create an interesting situation but not one that your rats will enjoy.

If you must transport your rat via the cargo hold of an airplane, consider the temperatures outside at the time of travel. Although the cargo hold temperature is normally animal friendly, the outside temperatures on the tarmac may not be.

Extreme temperatures could prove fatal to Ben and Ira. Make certain that your rat's carrier is airline approved. Attach some sort of identification card to the cage with your name, home address, and phone number as well as contact information while you're away from home. A padlock on the cage door is also a good idea, since you never know when curious people might try to open the cage for a quick look.

Make certain that your rat is comfortable in his carrier with clean, soft bedding; food; and a small water bottle filled with fresh water.

Prior to your trip, pack a kit for your rat. He will need wood chews, bedding, food, a scoop, plastic bags for cage cleanup, treats, toys, a harness and leash, and perhaps some vitamins such as Nutrical. I have found a portable exercise box such as Great Wall is a useful piece of travel gear. It's a rolled-up sheet of plastic that opens up into an exercise space large enough for you and many rats. While this may not be practical if traveling by air, you might have space for it in your vehicle.

Rat Shows

Rats are very popular pets, and several rat clubs currently sponsor well-organized shows for all varieties of rats. You can either participate in a rat show or just show up to cheer on your favorite variety. Either way, it's a fun activity you and your rat can share.

There are two types of rat shows: pet and variety. At a pet rat show, entries are judged more on personality than they are on appearance. They are also judged on their overall health, the cleanliness of their coats, and their appropriate weight and musculature, among other factors.

This rat impressed the judges.

The variety rat show has more divisions to accommodate the many rat "breeds," or standards. Each animal is judged as an individual representative of its standard. Thus, there are divisions for the Fancy, Rex, Velvet, Odd-Eyed, Tailless, Dumbo, and so on. The rats are judged on structure, color, coat, condition, personality, and behavior—judges do not look kindly on a rat that tries to escape or shows aggression.

Show Prep

Ever watch a dog or horse show? The exhibitors present clean, well-conditioned, and well-trained animals. This is no less the case at a rat show.

As a participant, you must bathe your rat, clip his nails, and make certain that his personality is well suited to show situations. Your pet cannot be shy or anxious. He must be in perfect physical condition without deformity of any sort.

When you fill out your entry form, be sure you enter Ira in the correct group or class. Entry in an inappropriate class is cause for disqualification and forfeit of the entry fee. Check out the specifications for each variety before filling out the entry form. Make certain that your rat fits those parameters as closely as possible. This will ensure entry and give your rat a chance to place in his class.

Debbie Ducommun's book *Rats* includes an excellent chapter on how to show your pets. If you are interested in this sport, I highly recommend this book and her suggestions for show preparation and exhibition. She's an expert on all things rat.

In recent years, outbreaks of viruses such as sialodacryoadentitis (SDA) and Sendai virus (SV) in rat colonies throughout the country have prompted the Rat and Mouse Club of America to urge rat owners not to take their rats to a show because of the risk of

A champion competitor rests atop his trophy.

contracting one of these contagious and fatal viruses. The Rat and Mouse Club considers the risk so high that it no longer sanctions shows. Before you fill out the entry form, therefore, weigh the issues of safety.

Unfortunately, inadequate or ineffective quarantine procedures (or lack thereof) continue to allow infected animals into the show environment, where the viruses may then spread to other participants. Therefore, exercise caution in deciding to show your rat—and do your homework. You can obtain more information about this at the Rat and Mouse Club of America Web site: www.rmca.org. The club not only tracks the virus outbreaks but also offers a huge amount of information about rat clubs all over the world.

Extreme Rat Challenge

Dr. Marty Klein began the Extreme Rat Challenge at Nebraska Wesleyan University in 1974. What began as a culmination of a basic learning principles course in the psychology department has since become the Xtreme Rat Challenge, an annual campus event that attracts widespread radio and television coverage, such as a segment on the Discovery Channel's *Wild Wild World*.

Each year, students are given a white laboratory rat and charged with teaching the rat some basic skills through operant conditioning techniques. The rats are taught to jump, run, climb, and lift weight. The trained rats then compete in five primary events: weightlifting, rope climb, long jump, hurdles, and tightrope. The students use stimuli such as sounds and lights to initiate the desired behavior. This is similar to your tapping to have your rat come to you—a visual and auditory stimulus.

In the tightrope event, the trainers and rats have three

chances to get the fastest crossing time. The time begins when the rat is put on the beginning of the platform and ends when the rat's nose reaches the end of the other platform.

In the rope climb, the rats are timed on how long it takes them to climb all the way up. The timer begins when the rat is placed on the bottom platform and ends when his nose reaches the top of the upper platform.

The hurdles are also timed. The rat contestants are let loose on a track with 2-inch hurdles, and the rat is given three chances to run entirely around. The fastest time wins. Observers can watch the rats run the track on a big-screen television.

The weightlifting event consists of a box with a lever on

You can set up your own challenges by building obstacle courses and timing your rats as they find their way through.

the inside. The weights are on the outside in a small bucket. The weights are 10 grams, 7 grams, and 3 grams. The scoring is based on the percentage of his body weight that the rat lifts.

The long jump is the toughest behavior to train. A rat is placed on a launching platform and must jump from a stand, without a moving start. He gets three minutes to perform the jump.

Rat Actors

Rats are showcased not only at rat shows, where the rodents are judged on appearance and personality, but also on screen as animal actors. Just think of the many movies and television shows that feature rats as either extras or leading characters. These rats had to undergo many months of training to perform in their acting roles. For film roles, several rats are typically trained to fill specific, specialized requirements. There are several Hollywood rat trainers who have provided rats for movies such as *2 Fast 2 Furious*, *Cats & Dogs*, *The Ring*, *Catwoman*, *Ben*, and *Total Recall*, among many others.

Boone Nar

One of the busiest animal trainers in California is Boone Nar. His animals have appeared in hundreds of feature films, including *The Year of the Rat*, *Pirates of the Caribbean*, *The Rock*, *Willard* (2003), *The Craft*, *The Green Mile*, *Edward Scissorhands*, and *Indiana Jones and the Last Crusade*. He provides all types of animal actors from exotics to dogs and cats; however, I single out these films as they all feature rats (or mice) in more than one scene.

Boone Nar prefers to provide well-trained and prepared animals to having many of the animal effects done with computer graphics. Often, a set is designed around his animal stars, and they are trained within that environment to promote a level of comfort and decrease the possibility of distraction while filming. However, animals can't always do what a director has in mind, so computer graphic imaging (CGI) is often used if a stunt might be too dangerous or impossible for a living creature.

Because of the magic of movies, a scene can be made to appear far different from reality. One example of this was a scene in *2 Fast 2 Furious* in which a man is being tortured with a rat on his chest. In the scene, a rat is put on the man's chest, a metal bucket is lowered over the rat, and a blowtorch is used to heat up the bucket. According to this plot, the rat becomes hot and claws the man's chest. There is even a shot that shows the rat inside the bucket. What actually occurred is hardly gruesome: a trained rat—Socrates, known for his role in the 2003 remake of the classic *Willard*—was placed inside the bucket. Prior to application of the blowtorch to the bucket, the rat was removed. For the shot in which the bucket is removed, the rat had been replaced. For the shot in which the rat is shown inside the bucket as the flames are surrounding him, CGI had been used in conjunction with images of Socrates, who had been trained to stand up on his hind legs and lean toward a large hole, which had been placed in the top of the bucket to allow a camera to peek inside. As Socrates had been trained to target on this hole, he automatically stood on his hind legs to reach upward.

Standing on an object can be one of a rat actor's trained behaviors for a scene.

In the movie *The One*, starring Jet Li, a rat was featured scampering out of a woman's high-heeled shoe wearing an antenna that detonates a bomb. This scene was produced by first attaching a lightweight antenna to the base of the rat's tail. The trainer then let the rat go from a hole in the floor under the shoe. When the rat was released, he followed a trail of baby food. Naturally, a fake rat was used for the explosion.

Samantha Martin

Samantha Martin runs an animal actors agency in the Midwest called Amazing Animals by Samantha. She got her start in the business by having rat actors available. Her love of rats began at the age of sixteen, when she walked into a pet shop and saw the playful rodents in their cages. As she was not allowed to have pets at the military school she attended, she kept her rat hidden. Her secret friend was soon found out, however, and moved to the science laboratory, where she visited him daily.

While employed at a pet shop, she worked with some cats, demonstrating how well the animals learned. This grabbed the attention of potential customers. As she had owned rats for several years, she decided to try the same techniques with them. Her Acrorat troop was born! Samantha's first business was The Rat Company. As she spent time training at the pet shop, she dreamed of a day when a producer would walk in, see what she had accomplished, and offer her a production job. Samantha's unlikely dream actually came true. Her first job was the independent film *Sam & Sara*. Her rats had to run across a field and climb into a box, and Samantha Martin was the rat and reptile wrangler.

The production was covered by a subsidiary of CNN and shown worldwide. A producer in Italy saw her work and hired her

Samantha Martin and her rat actors.

to perform in a holiday show. Her fame snowballed from there. She was featured on *Inside Edition, Early Edition, Geraldo,* and in extras on the DVD for the *Willard* remake. Her rats have appeared in several rat documentaries, entailing worldwide travel to places such as Austria. On one of her forays to Europe, her rats performed for Mino Damato, the Italian equivalent of David Letterman. While working in Los Angeles, she met Moe Disesso, who trained and provided the rats for the original *Willard* film in 1971.

Since becoming known as the Rat Lady, Samantha Martin has diversified to working with other animals, including cats, dogs, and small exotic mammals. Her main technique in rat performance involves the use of cues with a beeper. Initially, she pairs the beeper with the advent of food. All of her rats learn to come when they hear the beeper.

For the movie *Sam & Sara*, she taught several rats (she works with more than one at a time to compare rats' performance and abilities and select the best-qualified actors) to come to their travel crate, which contained the food, from farther and farther away—back chaining. In a short period of time, her rats could cross the field and climb into a box. Her food of choice for training and working through a production is Cocoa Krispies. The rats love it and eat it quickly. Plus, the cereal doesn't leave them too full to perform well.

When teaching her rats to move in a specific place, Samantha works with the back-chaining exercises and beeper. As they continually cross the surface, they leave their own scent trail, so there's no need to lay a path of smeared food to obtain the desired behavior.

Samantha uses a clicker when she has to teach very specific behaviors. One behavior chain she taught was for a rat to go into a burning dollhouse, bring out a doll, and place it in an ambulance. Working with several rats at the same time, she back chained the entire behavior sequence. She has discovered that competition drives rats to learn faster and perform more efficiently.

One of her early jobs was a comical television commercial for the Indiana Lottery. She provided eighteen rats that had to meander across the floor beneath some people who were tied up and forced to listen to awful music. Just beyond camera range was a hole in the wall of the set. Throughout the filming, the rats would disappear into this hole, and Samantha would pull them out. Upon completion of the job, she discovered she had five more rats than she started with! She decided to keep her new friends and put them to work in future productions. Looking back, she knew she should have blocked the hole. That would've saved her much anxiety and hard work.

Another interesting experience occurred while Samantha traveled in Italy. One of the rats' tricks was to ride around on remote-controlled cars. While she was going through a security checkpoint, the movement of the vehicle caused the toy cars to activate. Her vehicle was quickly surrounded by armed soldiers. An interesting but frightening experience.

As Samantha often travels overseas with her rats, she has to make certain to have health certificates and permits. On one occasion, she was separated from her rats as they were held up in Amsterdam, awaiting documentation, while she was already in Austria. That was one experience she doesn't wish to repeat. It was one thing to have her rats travel in the cargo areas but another thing entirely to be separated from them for two days as she dealt with the differing requirements from country to country.

Another precaution Samantha takes when traveling is labeling her animals "Long-Tailed Honduran Hamsters" instead of rats. This reduces the potential for incidents, as people are often repulsed by rats and alarmed by their presence.

Samantha uses specific sexes for specific jobs. Female rats are used for the live shows, since they are more energetic for longer periods of time and less likely to "leak." People also tend to be turned off by the male rat's larger and more menacing appearance. Because many movies use rats to establish an ominous mood, these male rats can come in handy. Her current movie project is a made-for-television horror flick titled *April Fools*. In this film, her rats have a simple, nonhorrifying job: run down an alley, a simple point-A-to-point-B behavior.

Samantha performs for hire with her female rats on Halloween. She lies in a casket as the rats run all over her body. Sound like a reality show? To someone who loves her rodents, it's loads of fun. What can be better than earning money while spending time with her friends?

Samantha's other rat production work includes the documentaries *Rat, Rat Among Us,* and *War Zone;* the feature films *Unconditional Love* and *The Evil One;* the television shows *Pet Star* and Animal Planet's *Wild on the Set;* music videos for Megadeth and Savatage; and commercials for breathmints and the Salvation Army.

Moe Disesso

Moe Disesso, the rat trainer for the original *Willard,* lived in Los Angeles before his recent death. He spent most of his life training rats—one at a time, unless the scene called for group action, in which case they were trained to perform their point-A-to-point-B motion as a unit. He too used a beeper to move the rats to their destination. While he was often impatient with humans, he had neverending patience for his rodent pupils.

Miriam Fields-Babineau (Author)

I have provided rats for television shows and a couple of movies. Each part required several months of preparation for all involved. I'll detail two of my jobs. The first was for a movie based on Edgar Allan Poe's "The Pit and the Pendulum," shown on The Learning Channel. The second was for an independent film. The Poe movie required some very natural rat behaviors—running around and chewing. The indie film, however, required many more hours of preparation, as the rat had to learn to wear a military outfit, with helmet, and salute on cue.

Here's what I did to prep the rats for the Poe movie. First, I had to find rats that looked like a wild Norway rat. This is a very

Moe Disesso and his famous rats.

large brown rat. Unfortunately, they're tough to find in a pet shop, so I settled for a couple of black rats, one gray, and one dark beige. (Prior to going on camera, each rat had to go through makeup to become brown!) They were males, so I didn't have to worry about mating during business hours. This also meant, however, that when they reached maturity there was a risk of more frequent rat fights. Needless to say, I obtained a very large, three-level cage for my rat actors so that they could exercise and remain in good condition as well as have their own space when they wished. Remember that a crowded cage will cause more scuffles than a roomy, multilevel cage.

I began by teaching all the rats to come when called for their breakfast lab block. This was easily learned, as they knew that not coming to the tap meant no breakfast. The only rat that offered any resistence was the beige rat, which was somewhat antisocial. The black rats were of the fancy variety and therefore very social and eager to learn. They had obviously received a lot of attention from a very young age. The gray rat began showing signs of illness shortly after I bought him, so I separated him from the others.

Each training session, I worked on teaching targeting and the *come* tap. I also conditioned the rats to follow a trail of mushed food. As one of their tasks was to appear to be chewing the ropes on the victim, they needed to really dig in with their teeth. The mushed food had to be rubbed in, but not so much that they would lose interest. Since the set was really an old operating theater in an abandoned veteran's hospital in Washington, D.C., there was a risk that the actors would run off instead of working. The rats had to be very interested in their rewards.

I had two assistants with me that day. It turned into a very dirty job as the floor had been gooped with spilled coffee, mud, moldy food, and other filth to portray an old dungeon. What was to be a simple job of having the rats remain on the actor's chest and chew the rope turned into a wild rodent chase as they became interested in all of the crazy smells around them. We completed the job in six hours, covered in filth and very tired. Who said Hollywood is glamorous? That certainly does not apply to the animal trainers!

Here's what I did to prep the rats for the indie film. I obtained a white laboratory rat and a black fancy rat. The white rat was for this indie film, and the black one was for another project. As both were very young when I bought them, I had thought it unnecessary to worry about their sex. Besides, the pet shop dealer told me they were both female. I should've checked for myself. It can be difficult for novice rat owners to recognize sex differences in young rats. I knew better but trusted this pet shop owner, since I had obtained many animals through him.

I spent at least an hour each day training the white rat to wear a GI Joe outfit and stand up on cue as well as to come to the tap. Two weeks before filming, the white rat started growing large. It was then that I noticed the black fancy rat was a male. He had barely begun to show the testicular sacs near his tail. I only hoped that the birthing day would not be on the same day as the filming. I lucked out; it occurred three days prior to production day. However, the mother rat had thirty babies! I have owned rats for most of my life but never saw a brood that large. (The average litter is eight.)

The way I acclimated the white rat to her outfit was to begin with the harness-training procedures. She learned to go into the costume in order to eat her dinner. Once she had it on, I began teaching her easy behaviors that she already knew well, such as to come to a tap and stand up. She quickly acclimated to the outfit, which sported a helmet and ammunition belt attached to a camouflage military shirt.

On production day, I brought mama and babies along with the costume we had been practicing with for a month. The rat was very comfortable in costume and didn't bat an eyelash at all the commotion involved in making a movie. She still had a large belly from carrying all those babies, but she performed like a soldier.

Your rat will be what you make of him. If you want someone to cuddle with while watching television, Ben will spend many hours snuggled close. Should you want an Acrorat like those of Samantha Martin, all it takes is a few minutes each day to train specific behaviors, best done around feeding time. If you want a traveling companion, rats are perfect as they require little time and space, giving you freedom to go wherever you wish.

Open your imagination, and let your rat shine.

10
Conclusion

Intelligent and affectionate, rats, especially well-trained ones, can make wonderful pets for the whole family.

IN THE LAST THREE DECADES, RATS HAVE MOVED FROM the laboratory into our homes as beloved pets. This is because they're easy to care for in many ways—they don't cost much to obtain or feed, they don't require as much time or financial commitment as a dog or cat does, and they are generally easy on people who might have pet-related allergies. Rats are interactive and affectionate. Rats are inquisitive and intelligent, making them easy to train. They interact well with other pets, if properly acclimated to one another. Rats can also be movie stars or star in their own "shows," whether rodent challenges or beauty contests.

Regardless of what you do with your pet rat, the more you teach him, the more interactive and intelligent the rat becomes. Rat training is the key to developing this relationship and maximizing your rodent's full potential.

Rat Clubs and Resources

Books

Bucsis, Gerry, and Barbara Somerville. 2000. *Training Your Pet Rat*. New York: Barron's.

Ducommun, Debbie. 2001. *Rats: Practical, Accurate Advice from the Expert*. Irvine, Calif.: BowTie Press.

Web Sites

The Agile Rat
www.fancyratagility.com

American Fancy Rat and Mouse Association
www.afrma.org

North American Rat and Mouse Club, International
www.narmci.8k.com

Onesta Organics
www.onestaorganics.com

The Rat Fan Club
www.ratfanclub.org

Rat and Mouse Club of America
www.rmca.org

Glossary

adaptable: able to exist in a new environment

back chaining: a training technique in which behaviors are taught in the reverse order of what is desired, with each behavior reinforced using the cue for the next

behavior chain: more than one trained behavior performed in a row

bumblefoot: an infection that occurs in rats and other rodents, marked by a red lesion on the foot

clicker: a mechanical device that makes a click sound to tell your rat exactly when he is doing the right thing

colony: multiple individuals of the same species sharing the same habitat

criteria: the rules of the routine (e.g., how long it should take)

cue: a signal—visual, verbal, or scent based—given to the rat to perform a desired behavior

fancy: word used to describe the varieties of rats promoted by breeders for pet and show purposes

habitat: the living environment

hierarchy: pecking order, the rat's rank in the colony

lure: an enticing piece of food that captures your rat's attention; can also be a tap or a stick

mark: a specific sound that translates to the receipt of a reward; *see clicker*

marker: a piece of cloth that the rat learns to go to and remain on until he receives his marker for rewards

motivator: a type of food that the rat really likes and will work for (not his usual lab block)

neutral territory: a place where no rat has been for any length of time and so does not harbor any scent

nocturnal: more active at night

operant conditioning: the teaching of a behavior in response to the presentation of a stimulus, such as a cue, and the subsequent rewarding of that behavior

positive reinforcement: giving rewards for doing as requested

regress: not performing as previously; the opposite of progress

response: the behavior exhibited at the presentation of a cue

Sendai virus (SV): a common and serious respiratory disease in rodents, similar to influenza

sialodacryoadentitis (SDA): a deadly and highly contagious virus in rats that weakens the immune system

stimuli: cues or objects presented to the rat to obtain a response

target stick: a stick with a small ball or other focal point on the tip, used to bring the rat's attention to a particular location

Index

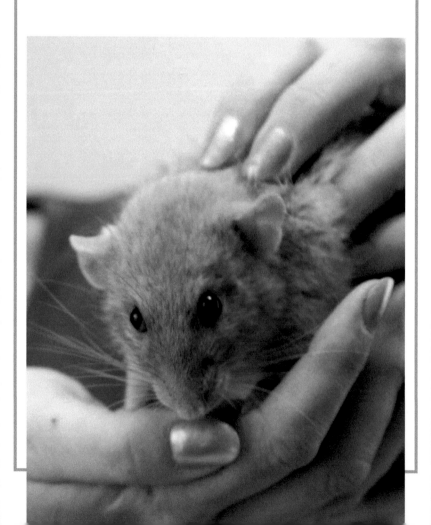